CLARENDON LIBRARY OF LOGIC AND PHILOSOPHY
General Editor: L. Jonathan Cohen

INTERESTS AND RIGHTS

ALSO PUBLISHED IN THIS SERIES

INTERESTS AND RIGHTS

The Case Against Animals

R. G. FREY

CLARENDON PRESS · OXFORD
1980

Oxford University Press, Walton Street, Oxford OX2 6DP

OXFORD LONDON GLASGOW
NEW YORK TORONTO MELBOURNE WELLINGTON
KUALA LUMPUR SINGAPORE JAKARTA HONG KONG TOKYO
DELHI BOMBAY CALCUTTA MADRAS KARACHI
NAIROBI DAR ES SALAAM CAPE TOWN

Published in the United States by
Oxford University Press, New York

British Library Cataloguing in Publication Data
Frey, R G
   Interests and rights. – (Clarendon Library of
   logic and philosophy).
   1. Animals, Treatment of – Moral and religious
   aspects
   I. Title
   170   HV4708   79–41385
   ISBN 0–19–824421–5

Set by Hope Services, Abingdon.
Printed & Bound by
Billing & Sons Ltd.,
Guildford, Worcester,
London, Oxford

Preface

To many, this book may be upsetting. For in its way it con-
tests the current and, I know, deeply felt philosophical
orthodoxy on rights, animals, and vegetarianism. So far as I
am aware, it is unique in this respect, a claim which I intend
not as a boast but rather as an indication of the pervasiveness
of this orthodoxy. In view of this, I must plead with the
reader to give the book's case a chance; my hope is that it
will grow on him. I have tried hard to assist this growth: the
book is short, carefully structured and argued throughout,
and I have striven rigorously to exclude everything, including
discussion of otherwise important issues, which is not absolutely directly connected with its central theme, as set out in
the Introduction.

I have sub-titled the book 'The Case Against Animals'
because that accurately reflects both the direction in which
its arguments point and the nature of the conclusions it
reaches; but I have not included this phrase as part of the
title itself because the discussions here of rights, interests,
needs, desires, beliefs, language, emotions, reasons, etc. are
not relevant or applicable only to the case of animals but are
of wider import.

The footnotes are important. They do indicate what I
have read in connection with particular points and so use-
fully reference what a mere collection of titles in a biblio-
graphy could not hope similarly to achieve. But I have also
used the notes to help provide perspective to the text, to
enable the reader not only to deepen his reading on some
particular point but also to deepen it often in a way different
from, often in a way at odds with my discussion of that point.

At a number of points in the text, the reader may well
expect a digression into a consideration of some part or other
of utilitarian theory. With the exception of Chapters I, IV,
and X, however, which in fact are connected to my central

theme, all such considerations have been expunged, in accordance with the policy stated above. Some appear in my book *Aspects of Consequentialism*, a defence of a consequentialist theory of rightness, now being revised for publication; others must await another occasion.

I have had the good fortune to be able to read most of this book in the form of papers to discussion groups, university audiences, and popular as well as learned societies, and I have nearly always learned from the ensuing discussions, for which I am grateful. Some of these occasions warrant particular mention.

A much condensed version of Chapter IV was read to a conference at Trinity College, Cambridge, on The Rights of Animals, at which I had an opportunity to meet with and talk to many of the people active in this area, such as Stephen Clark, Andrew Linzey, Mary Midgley, my old friend Tom Regan, Richard Ryder, Timothy Sprigge, and countless others. After my paper, the distinguished ethologist W.H. Thorpe asked me several questions in connection with my view that animals lack beliefs, which I was really unable to answer except in the most tentative fashion; my answers now appear in Chapters VI, VII, VIII, and IX. An earlier version of Chapter VI was read to The Bertrand Russell Society, at a recent meeting of the Eastern Division of the American Philosophical Association. Several members of the audience later, over dinner, quizzed me so thoroughly in connection with it that it, together with the sections on needs and desires in Chapter VII, has profited enormously as a result. Many kind people in Göttingen and Berlin discussed parts of this book with me, and I am especially grateful to the University of Göttingen and to the Philosophisch-Politische Akademie E. v. Sitz Kassel for enabling me to air a much earlier version of Chapter VII and my, I'm afraid, not very popular views on Leonard Nelson, as found, for example, in Chapter V. Some remarks by Keith Lehrer in Göttingen gave me the idea on how to develop the first part of Chapter VIII, and discussions with Heinrich Müller in Berlin and Michael A. Fox in Cambridge have enabled me to tighten up parts of Chapters IV and IX. In different versions, Chapter XI, an extended critique of Peter Singer's case for vegetarianism, has been read a number of times, including to the University of Liverpool, as a Monday Lecture, and to several gatherings of vegetarians in the United States, at which its reception was what I can best describe as wildly animated.

A number of people have read this book in its entirety, and I should like especially to thank John Benson, Peter Singer, and L. Jonathan Cohen for their very helpful written remarks and suggestions. Tom Regan and Clara Weininger have given me their reactions to earlier versions of Chapter XI. Parts of Chapters I, II, IV and X stem from work which I did at Oxford under R.M. Hare.

Debts of a general kind in philosophy I owe to many people in Oxford, but especially to R.M. Hare and P.M.S. Hacker, from both of whom, first as student, then as friend, I have learned a great deal.

I have also to thank Bobbie Matthews for her highly intelligent reading of my script and for her rapid and skilful typing of this book.

I dedicate this work to my father, who in every way at his disposal has assisted and supported me throughout my life, and to the memory of my mother, whose death has deprived all who knew her of so very much.

November 1978   R. G. F.

Acknowledgements

Some of the material presented here has appeared in notes and articles by me, and I wish to thank the editors and publishers of *Analysis* ('Animal Rights', 37, 1977), *American Philosophical Quarterly* ('Rights, Interests, Desires and Beliefs', 16, 1979), and *The Philosophical Quarterly* ('Interests and Animal Rights', 27, 1977), as well as the RSPCA and the Centaur Press of Sussex ('What has Sentiency to do with the Possession of Rights?', in *Animals' Rights — A Symposium*, eds' D. Paterson, R. Ryder, 1979) and Felix Meiner Verlag of Hamburg ('Leonard Nelson and the Moral Rights of Animals', in *Vernunft — Erkenntnis — Sittlichkeit,* ed. P. Schröder, 1979), for permitting me to draw upon some of this material again. I should add, however, that I have not hesitated to alter and completely re-arrange this material, in order better to develop my case here.

Contents

Introduction

Perhaps the most significant development in moral philosophy over the past few years has been the increasing attention devoted to practical questions and to practical applications of philosophy. One result has been that the subjects of animal rights and vegetarianism have once again come before the philosophical public as proper topics of debate, and a flood of material has been released. True, I here further inundate this public; but I do so with a difference. For unlike virtually everyone else who has contributed to these debates, I propose to cast doubt upon the claims that animals possess moral rights and that vegetarianism possesses a moral basis. In fact, I think both these claims false; but to establish this conclusively I should have to go through the numerous grounds which have been proposed for their truth, and no publisher is likely to prove so indulgent, even if he could afford to. What I have done, therefore, is to select one of the most widely influential grounds for the alleged truth of both claims and to criticize it, with a view to showing both that and why it will not do. Nevertheless, I comment, sometimes at length, upon a number of other grounds in the course of thoroughly examining this one; and my criticisms in each case stand on their own.

The ground in question consists in the claim that animals have interests, and the linkage between this claim and the subjects of moral rights for animals and vegetarianism is straightforward. It has often been suggested that only beings which possess interests can possess moral rights, and attention quite naturally comes to focus, therefore, upon whether animals have interests; and on the basis of the claim that animals do have interests, it has recently been argued, for example by Peter Singer, that the moral principle of the equal consideration of interests applies to them and requires that we become vegetarians. These two positions are distinct, since it does not follow in the least that the vegetarian who bases his position ultimately upon animal interests is committed to the view that animals possess moral rights. But both positions turn upon the claim that animals do have interests, and I shall argue not only that the writers considered have failed to establish the truth of this claim but also that the claim itself is simply false. The central argument by which I try to achieve this latter objective — about the relation between interests and needs, desires, beliefs, language, emotions, and reasons for action on the one hand and between interests and sentience on the other — is the central argument of the book, and it will, I think, be of interest even to those who have no especial concern with animal rights and related issues. Certainly, it will be evident throughout that I have these other readers in mind.

I support wholeheartedly the application of philosophy to practical issues; but it is as well to be aware at the outset of the form which the philosopher's contribution to these issues takes. It is, as R.M. Hare has impressed upon me, simply this: philosophy is concerned with testing arguments for soundness, and the occupation of the philosopher is to carry out this testing. To this end, he deploys the tools and canons of logic on behalf of accuracy in argument, explores questions of meaning, implication, presupposition, derivation, relation, compatibility, etc., pries into and generates examples and counter-examples, both realistic and hypothetical, and so on. One but only one of the tools he deploys in this task is the analysis of those concepts in which the arguments he is testing are set out; analysis is not, however, an alternative view of what the philosopher is about, in some way competing with his assessment of arguments. By contrast, though he can and doubtless should concern himself with and even soak himself in the factual material pertaining to the specific arguments under his gaze, further increases in this factual material and knowledge are not part of the philosopher's task as such. The philosophical case against the ascription of interests (and thereby moral rights) to animals to be presented here does not turn, for example, upon any new and important facts of animal behaviour which I have uncovered and of which others are ignorant. If anything, it turns upon an analysis of what it is to have interests, desires, beliefs, etc., together with an examination of arguments for animal rights and vegetarianism which incorporate or rely upon these notions. Empirical observations, empirical studies matter, of course, as we shall see; but it is not by factual information of this sort that I hope to deprive the claims that animals possess moral rights and that vegetarianism has a moral basis of their alleged foundation in the possession of interests.

Unlike others writing in this area, therefore, my aim is not to convert; it is rather to engender and foster a critical attitude towards the arguments by which they would convert us. Strength of conviction is a wonderful thing, but only if the conviction has been thoroughly tested for soundness. And thoroughly testing for soundness, I think, is the philosopher's *raison d'être*.

I

Moral Rights:
Some Doubts

The question of whether non-human animals possess moral rights is once again being widely argued. Doubtless the rise of ethology is partly responsible for this: as we learn more about the behaviour of animals, it seems inevitable that we shall be led to focus upon the similarities between them and us, with the result that the extension of moral rights from human beings to non-human animals can appear, as the result of these similarities, to have a firm basis in nature. But the major impetus to renewed interest in the subject of animal rights almost certainly stems from a heightened and more critical awareness, among philosophers and non-philosophers alike, of the arguments for and against eating animals and using them in scientific research. For if animals *do* have moral rights, such as a right to live and to live free from unnecessary suffering, and if our present practices systematically tread upon these rights, then the case for eating and experimenting upon animals, especially when other alternatives are for the most part readily available, is going to have to be a powerful one indeed.

It is important, however, not to misconstrue the question: the question is not about *which* rights animals may or may not be thought to possess or about whether their alleged rights in a particular regard are on a par with the alleged rights of humans in this same regard but rather about the more fundamental issue of whether animals — or, in any event, the 'higher' animals — can be the logical subject of rights.

One enormously influential position on this issue is that

which links the possession of rights to the possession of interests. In *A System of Ethics*, Leonard Nelson is among the first, if not the first, to propound the view that all and only beings which have interests can have rights,[1] a view which has attracted an increasingly wide following ever since. For example, in recent years, H.J. McCloskey has embraced this view but gone on to deny that animals have interests,[2] whereas Joel Feinberg has embraced the view but gone on to affirm that animals have interests.[3] Nelson himself is emphatic that animals as well as human beings are, as he puts it, 'carriers of interests',[4] and he concludes, accordingly, that animals possess moral rights, rights which both deserve and warrant our respect. For Nelson, then, it is because animals have interests that they can be the logical subject of rights, and his claim that animals *do possess* interests forms the minor premiss, therefore, in an argument for the moral rights of animals:

All and only beings which (can) have interests (can) have moral rights;
Animals as well as humans (can) have interests;
Therefore, animals (can) have moral rights.

McCloskey, Feinberg, and a host of others have accepted the major premiss of this argument, which I shall dub the interest requirement, but have disagreed over the truth of the minor premiss; and it is apparent that the minor premiss is indeed the key to the whole matter. For given the truth of the interest requirement, it is still the case that only the truth of the minor premiss would result in the inclusion of creatures other than human beings within the class of right-holders. Accordingly, since I desire to meet and confound my opponents on their own ground, it is the minor premiss of this

---

[1] Leonard Nelson, *A System of Ethics*, trans. Norbert Guterman (Yale University Press, New Haven, 1956), Part I, Section 2, Ch. 7, pp. 136-44. See T. Regan, 'Introduction', in *Animal Rights and Human Obligations*, ed. T. Regan, P. Singer (Prentice-Hall, Englewood Cliffs, N.J., 1976), pp. 16 f. See also J. Passmore, *Man's Responsibility for Nature* (Duckworth, London, 1974), pp. 113-16.

[2] H.J. McCloskey, 'Rights', *Philosophical Quarterly*, 15 (1965), 115-27.

[3] J. Feinberg, 'The Rights of Animals and Unborn Generations', in *Philosophy and Environmental Crisis*, ed. W.T. Blackstone (University of Georgia Press, Athens, Georgia, 1974), pp. 43-68.

[4] Op. cit. 138.

argument which will concern me. But, first, there are two aspects of the major premiss that warrant attention, the second of which raises very large and important issues.

The major premiss as given by Nelson and endorsed by McCloskey and Feinberg does not show that the possession of interests is a necessary and sufficient condition for the possession of moral rights but simply states that it is, and it is as well to bear in mind that other suggestions in this regard are thick on the ground. The possession of rationality, language, free will, choice, and culture; the capacity to experience pain, to recognize and discharge moral obligations; the acceptance of and participation within societal and communal relationships; these have all at one time or another had their advocates. (I shall return to several of these later.) It is not that the presence of so many suggested necessary (and perhaps also sufficient) conditions for the possession of moral rights *shows* that none of these is in fact such a condition; it is rather that the extent and variety of suggestions serves as a useful antidote to any unthinking presumption that the major premiss of Nelson's argument really does encapsulate a necessary and sufficient condition for the possession of moral rights. Perhaps it does; but it is at least not obvious that it does.

More importantly, however, the major premiss implicitly assumes that there are moral rights, and it is not at all clear to me that there are.[5] The same assumption is made when it is asked, as it constantly is today, whether there are some moral rights, such as a right to live and to live free from unnecessary

---

[5] There are, of course, institutional rights within social institutions, such as promising and marriage; and if one regards these social institutions wherein quasi-contracts are made as moral institutions as well, then these institutional rights are also moral ones. I am not here concerned with quasi-contractual arrangements of this sort. No one to my knowledge presently argues for an animal's supposed moral right to live and to live free from unnecessary suffering or a woman's supposed moral right to an abortion on demand on this basis.

I do not mean to imply here, of course, that other philosophers have not their doubts about moral rights as well. In this regard, and relevant to my general position in this chapter, see the very useful articles by John Kleinig, 'Human Rights, Legal Rights and Social Change', in *Human Rights*, eds. E. Kamenka, A. Tay (Edward Arnold, London, 1978), pp. 36–47, and Robert Young, 'Dispensing With Moral Rights', *Political Theory*, 6 (1978), 63–74. See also R.M. Hare's well-known piece 'Abortion and the Golden Rule', *Philosophy and Public Affairs*, 4 (1975), 2 ff.

suffering, which can be extended from human beings to animals. The history of ethics reveals, however, that it is by no means an easy task to show that human beings do possess moral rights. And if they do not, then the question of the extension of such rights from humans to animals does not arise; there is, so to speak, nothing to extend. Arguments for animal rights which either explicitly or implicitly turn upon such an extension will accordingly be vitiated.

Of course, talk of moral rights and their more fashionable variants, such as women's rights, children's rights, animal rights, environmental rights, etc., is rife, and scarcely a day passes without some such alleged right being in the news. But are there really any moral rights? Not even philosophers have been liberal with arguments to show that there are. For example, in *Taking Rights Seriously*,[6] Ronald Dworkin claims that each of us has an absolutely fundamental political or moral right to equal concern and respect, a right which is not created by or the product of community legislation or social practice, which persists even in the face of contrary legislation or practice, and which prescribes the boundary beyond which neither individuals nor the community may go in pursuit of their over-all ends. But is there really such a fundamental moral right? I cannot find Dworkin's argument to show that there is. Rather, he simply says he is going to take this right to equal concern and respect 'to be fundamental and axiomatic',[7] an axiom which, since claims to moral rights now enjoy such wide favour, doubtless many of his readers will accept.

Indeed, I suspect at large, in public affairs, the burden of proof has in a quiet way been shifted from the shoulders of those who claim that there is this or that moral right on to the shoulders of those who doubt that this is so. A contemporary of mine at Oxford has enjoyed considerable success (and some notoriety) in the United States in his campaign to have smoking in public places banned. He claims we have a moral right to breathe clean air, which he in turn uses to justify his demand that smoking in public places be made a

---

[6] R. Dworkin, *Taking Rights Seriously* (Duckworth, London, 1977).
[7] Ibid. xv. For a stimulating and critical discussion of Dworkin on rights, see Joseph Raz's review in *Political Studies*, xxvi (1978), 123–37.

legal offence; and he has successfully put on the defensive
those of his opponents who doubt that we have such a right.
After all, who wants to be portrayed in public, perhaps in the
context of a municipal election, as defending some form or
other of what my friend is bound to label as pollution. (And
this is how one will be portrayed: as I have found to my
cost, in reading papers on the subject of animal rights, to
query whether animals are the possessors of rights is inevitably portrayed as defending, if not advocating, cruelty
towards them.)

My reason for doubting that there are any moral rights is
perfectly straightforward and can be briefly put.

What is it to have a right? Doubtless the most prominent
answer to this question today is Joel Feinberg's, as set out in
his papers 'Duties, Rights and Claims'[8] and 'The Nature and
Value of Rights'.[9] To have a right, according to Feinberg,
whose answer is drawn up around the notion of a legal right,
is to have a claim to something or against others. To have a
legal right to the collection of rent is to have a claim to
prompt payment from one's tenants; to have a legal right to
privacy in one's home is to have a claim against others not to
invade one's privacy through trespass, and so on. Thus, to
have a legal right is to be able to make claims, claims which
can be enforced, which one can properly insist upon having
enforced, and which the courts, properly petitioned, will see
are enforced. In this way, being able to make claims, enforced and backed by sanctions, forms an important part of
what it is for a person to function in society, which is why
the deprivation of one's legal rights, as in the case, for instance, of some Soviet dissidents, is such a severe loss, even
though one remains at liberty in society.

But what if one lacks the ability to make claims at all?
This problem, obviously of concern, for example, to animal
and environmental rightists, since neither dogs nor trees can
make or insist upon or petition the courts on behalf of their
claims, is held to be solved by appealing to the cases of small

[8] J. Feinberg, 'Duties, Rights and Claims', *American Philosophical Quarterly*,
iv (1966), 137-44.
[9] J. Feinberg, 'The Nature and Value of Rights', *Journal of Value Inquiry*, iv
(1970), 243-60.

children, the very seriously infirm, and the mentally sub-normal, all of whom are conceded legal rights but in respect of whom the courts, if necessary, appoint persons to make and exercise claims and to petition for legal proceedings on their behalf. It is arguable that nothing prevents a similar treatment of dogs[10] and trees.[11]

Though Feinberg's analysis of rights is drawn up with legal rights in mind, it is widely extended to morals, and Feinberg himself so extends it in 'The Nature and Value of Rights'.[12] This extension has recently been criticized by William Nelson, on the ground that, in order to be extended, there must be an activity in morals comparable to that of making claims in the case of legal rights and in which right-holders alone can properly participate; and Nelson argues, convincingly, I think, that the legal and moral cases are unlike in this respect.[13] I want to explore a different aspect of Feinberg's analysis, one which, when the analysis is applied to morals, leads to the conclusion that claims to moral rights do not play the serious and decisive role that claims to rights play in law. There are two ways of showing this, though, as will be seen, they are connected; the first leads to the view that moral rights are superfluous, and the second, issuing out of the first, leads to the view that we cannot affirm that there are any moral rights.

[10] Cf. J. Feinberg, 'The Rights of Animals and Unborn Generations', pp. 46 ff.; Regan, in *Animal Rights and Human Obligations*, p. 15.

[11] Cf. C. Stone, *Should Trees Have Standing? Toward Legal Rights for Natural Objects* (Avon Books, New York, 1975), especially Ch. 2. In the United States, the remarks of Justice William O. Douglas, in the important US Supreme Court decision in *Sierra Club* v. *Morton* [405 U.S. 727, 1972], in which reference was made to Stone's work, aided enormously in popularizing the movement for extending legal and moral rights to natural objects. For an important and penetrating critical discussion of Stone, see John Rodman, 'The Liberation of Nature?', *Inquiry*, 20 (1977), 83-131. See also the following exchange: L.H. Tribe, 'Ways Not to Think about Plastic Trees: New Foundations for Environmental Law', 83 *Yale Law Journal* 1315 (1974); M. Sagoff, 'On Preserving the Natural Environment', 84 *Yale Law Journal* 205 (1974); and L.H. Tribe, 'From Environmental Foundations to Constitutional Structures: Learning from Nature's Future', 84 *Yale Law Journal* 480 (1975). For a discussion of this exchange by an animal rightist, see S.R.L. Clark's major work *The Moral Status of Animals* (Clarendon Press, Oxford, 1977), pp. 164 ff. For Clark's views on conservation and the environment, see especially his Ch. VIII.

[12] 249 ff.

[13] W. Nelson, 'On the Alleged Importance of Moral Rights', *Ratio*, xviii (1976), 145-55.

To have a legal right to the collection of rent is to have a claim to prompt payment from one's tenants; but it is not only this. It is also, as Feinberg is aware, to have a claim that is justified. What justifies one's claim to the collection of rent are the terms of the lease, contract, or certificate of agreement which has been agreed between one's tenants or their agents and oneself and which is legally enforceable, except in certain specifiable circumstances, in the courts. Suppose, then, that a feminist claims that women have a moral right to abortion on demand: what must confer this right upon women, since there is no agreed contractual arrangement (either implicit or explicit) between society and individual women which does, must be some moral principle or other which is alleged by the feminist to be the ground of this right. A principle to the effect that it is wrong to interfere with a woman's control or power over her own body is, for example, one possibility sometimes suggested in this regard; and what the feminist is ultimately claiming is that this principle justifies her claim to an abortion on demand.

Thus, if we challenge the claim that women have such a right, what we find ourselves arguing about with the feminist is the moral principle which is alleged by her to be the ground of this right; and what ends up being in dispute between us is the acceptability of this principle. Its acceptability is everything: you are only going to accept that women have a moral right to abortion on demand if you accept the moral principle which is alleged to confer this right upon them. There are five aspects to this argument between the feminist and ourselves to which attention must be drawn.

(1) What we are arguing about is not the right but the ground of the right, the particular moral principle appealed to; and the point at issue between us is the acceptability of this principle. Not to accept it, given it is the ground of the right, is effectively to deny that women have the right in question.

(2) It is a plain fact that there is widespread disagreement over moral principles, whether or not they are cited as the alleged ground of some moral right. It is not at all obvious that women have a moral right to an abortion on demand,

and anyone who thought that the moral principle (or that interpretation of it) which is alleged to confer this right upon women commanded widespread assent would be deceiving themselves. One need only reflect on the widespread disagreement there is over sexual morality in order to see how little agreement in moral principles there very often is.

(3) Worse yet, there is widespread disagreement among us even about the very canons of acceptability in moral principles. Some philosophers have sought formal criteria of acceptability, others material; some have cited agreement with the convictions of the 'plain man', others agreement with some specific subset of these convictions which can be rationally based; some have cited the achievement of a condition of reflective equilibrium between our principles and our judgements, while others have dismissed this as but a sophisticated version of intuitionism. The feminist will not be allowed merely to suppose that some moral principle is acceptable, she must show that it is; but then she faces the difficulty that the criteria of acceptability in moral principles are not settled and agreed among us, as anyone who places a principle of utility among these criteria and anyone who does not can easily attest.

On the basis of these three aspects of our argument with the feminist, a fourth can now be seen in the proper perspective.

(4) Argument can and does proceed about moral principles and their acceptability *whether or not* there are rights allegedly grounded upon them. Indeed, even in a world devoid of moral rights, argument of this sort can easily occur. Thus, we can argue about the acceptability of a principle which gives a woman absolute control or power over her own body, even when a foetus is present in it, whether or not we posit some moral right to an abortion on demand grounded upon it. Likewise, we can argue about whether a moral principle in respect of killing applies to animals even if animals are accorded no moral rights whatever; and *we have to argue* about this principle and its acceptability in any event, if you seek to endow animals with a right to life on its basis. The point, then, is an important one *vis-à-vis* claims to moral rights: if such claims are made, then we have to argue about the principles cited as their ground; if such claims are not

made, we can still argue about these and other moral principles of rightness and justification of treatment. It is not as if the making of such claims is what opens up the possibility of argument about the moral principles in which they are allegedly grounded.

On the basis of these four aspects of our argument with the feminist, a fifth can now be seen in the form of a conclusion.

(5) If we do reach agreement on canons of acceptability in moral principles, and if we do then reach agreement in moral principles, what is the point of going on to posit this or that moral right? For if we take morality seriously and try to put our principles into action, we shall change our behaviour to accord with our principles. To posit a moral right in addition seems a superfluous gesture. If we cannot reach agreement of the sorts described, we are not going to agree about whether there is such a right in the first place; and if we do reach agreement of the sorts described, there no longer is a need to postulate the existence of a right, since my moral principles will now direct me to act in ways perhaps different from those in which I have been acting. So far as I can see, not even a practical advantage[14] is gained by positing some moral right based upon agreed moral principles, since I as a moral man, implementing and following my principles, will behave the way you want me to *even without the right.*

On this argument, the conclusion in respect of the extension of Feinberg's analysis of rights to morals is that claims to rights do not play the serious and decisive role in morals which they play in law but rather appear to lead nowhere. For if they are put forward on the basis of unagreed moral principles, we will not agree on whether there are such rights, which is presently the case; whereas if they are put forward on the basis of agreed moral principles, they appear to have become superfluous and to have lost whatever initial advantage — putting one's opponents on the defensive, as with my friend who wants to ban smoking — they sometimes gain for their proponents.

If I am right, however, what task *is* the phrase 'have a right' performing in the sentence 'Women have a right to

[14] See R. Young, 'Dispensing With Moral Rights', 69.

abortion on demand'? It performs, I suggest, two tasks. First, it serves as a reminder that, in discussing abortion, we must not concentrate upon the foetus to the exclusion of the woman, must not pay attention to the interests of the foetus or of the child the foetus will become at the expense of attention to the interests of the woman. For abortion affects not only the foetus but also, and equally importantly, the woman. Essentially, this amounts to using claims to moral rights as a way of trying to focus attention upon the woman, as a way of trying to keep before one's opponents and to impress upon them considerations about the woman's interests which one fears they will otherwise lose sight of. In other words, claims to moral rights are being used to draw attention to the presence of interests, which must not be ignored. As such, claims of this sort have doubtless proved helpful to feminists and others, even though it is true that we can easily draw attention to the interests of the woman in abortion situations and to the effects of many of our practices upon animals without employing claims to moral rights at all; indeed, virtually all utilitarians already do so, as Jonathan Glover illustrates in respect of abortion in his *Causing Death and Saving Lives*[15] and Peter Singer illustrates in respect of animals in his *Animal Liberation*.[16] Second, and as is widely accepted today, the phrase 'have a right' also records the fact that she who claims that 'Women have a right to abortion on demand' considers it to be morally wrong or unjustified to deprive a woman of an abortion when she wants one.

Interestingly, feminists widely use as a way of rallying their supporters the cry 'Women ought to have the right to abortion on demand' (or, less commonly, 'Women should be able to have an abortion when they want one'); but this way of putting the matter makes it quite clear, I think, that women are not being credited with 'having the right' to an abortion on demand. In fact the cry 'Women ought to have the right to abortion on demand' strikes me as pointing away from morals and moral rights and towards the law and legal rights; it is maintaining, I think, that legislation ought to be

[15] J. Glover, *Causing Death and Saving Lives* (Penguin Books, Harmondsworth, Middlesex, 1977).
[16] P. Singer, *Animal Liberation* (Jonathan Cape, London, 1976).

enacted — among other reasons, because it is thought morally wrong (at the very least, by the feminist) to deprive a woman of an abortion when she wants one — so that women come to enjoy the *legal right* to abortion on demand.

Now though the feminist thinks it morally wrong to deprive a woman of an abortion on demand, a good many other people do not; and this is the point from which my second argument to show that claims to rights in morals do not play the serious and decisive role they play in law begins. *Per se*, such clashes in moral judgements are common and, philosophically, rather uninteresting; where they become interesting, as should be clear from my first argument, is when we attempt to arbitrate them by trying to come up with theses or standards of rightness, wrongness, and justification. For what we find when we try to do this is that these theses and standards are themselves in dispute; and since they are dependent upon the normative ethical theory we embrace, it follows that it is *the adequacy* of such theories which is really in dispute between us and which we find it difficult to deal with.

What I have in mind here can be illustrated from my own case. Following G.E. Moore, we can distinguish between the following questions:

(1) What does 'right' mean?
(2) Which acts are right?[17]

If (1) is a meta-ethical question, then (2) is a normative ethical question; for in order to be able to answer (2), at least if we are going to be in anything like a sufficiently strong position from which to defend our answers to (2), we must also be in a position to answer this question:

(3) What makes right acts right?

And (3) is, I should stress, a question of theory, the answer to which is supplied by a normative ethical theory. For example, I consider myself to be some sort of act-utilitarian; I subscribe, therefore, to the view that acts are right or wrong

---

[17] For an important discussion of this distinction, which is relevant to my concerns here, see R.M. Hare, 'The Argument from Received Opinion', in *Essays in Philosophical Method* (Macmillan, London, 1971), pp. 117–35.

solely in virtue of the goodness or badness of their consequences. This means that I am a consequentialist, in that I
hold that what makes right acts right are their (actual) consequences. Consequential/act-utilitarianism, then, provides me
with *a way of* answering (2): I find out which particular acts
are right by assessing their individual consequences. It is not,
therefore, my answers to (2) but my answer to (3) *that is
crucial*; for my answers to (2) — my specific moral judgements about what is right and wrong and justified — are but a
direct outcome of the application of the theory I espouse in
respect of (3). Thus, the acceptability or adequacy of my
normative ethic is of vital concern; for the only way *I can
defend my answers to (2)*, when their critical evaluation is
undertaken, is by showing that they have been arrived at by
the consistent application of my act-utilitarianism and by
then trying to defend my act-utilitarianism. Since my normative ethical views depend upon my normative ethical theory,
to query me on the worth of the one without querying me
on the adequacy of the other is pointless. But how do we tell
whether a normative ethical theory is adequate? Or whether
it is perhaps more adequate than certain rival theories? These
are by no means easy questions; certainly, as is well known
and long bemoaned in the literature, there are no agreed
answers to them, which explains the otherwise curious fact
that act-utilitarians and their critics, in spite of numerous
differences in theory and practice, each continue to flourish.
Yet such questions must be addressed and answered, I think,
if one's own or one's group's moral convictions about the
rightness or wrongness or justification of this or that are to
be given or considered to have pre-eminent weight. For if
one's moral judgements in these respects ultimately reflect
one's normative ethical theory, then unless one can show
that this underlying theory is adequate, why should one's
own or one's group's moral judgements be given or considered
to have pre-eminent weight, for example, first in making a
case for and then in framing a law which allows abortion on
demand? In the absence of such demonstrative adequacy of
theory, why *should* a feminist's judgement about the moral
rightness of abortion on demand be given pride of place in
this way? Certainly, her opponents are exceedingly unlikely

to give way under such a condition.

What must be done, then, is that the feminist must show that, once a test of adequacy has been devised and agreed upon, her normative ethical theory, which *inter alia* confers a moral right on women to abortion on demand, can satisfy this test. Three additional points are noteworthy in this regard. First, I say an 'agreed' test of adequacy because, otherwise, we are unlikely to agree either as to the adequacy of the theory in question or as to the moral rights which are alleged to find their ground in it. Second, we cannot exclude *a priori* the intriguing, if perplexing, possibility that, given a test of adequacy is at last devised and agreed upon, at least two normative ethical theories satisfy it, one of which confers upon women the moral right to an abortion on demand, the other of which explicitly does not. Third, the best-known test of adequacy, historically, is now widely rejected. Agreement with received opinion or ordinary moral convictions or the views of the 'plain man', or some particular subset of these opinions, convictions, or views, is no longer widely endorsed as the test of adequacy for a normative ethical theory;[18] and loud echoes of its rejection can be heard in the protests — those of R. M. Hare[19] and of Peter Singer[20] immediately come to mind — provoked by the similar test adopted by John Rawls in *A Theory of Justice,* viz., of acceptability to us under a condition of reflective equilibrium.[21] These protests alone should show how highly contentious this issue of adequacy is and so how very unhelpful it is for a feminist merely to postulate the adequacy of some theory by which to obtain the result, i.e. that women have a moral right to abortion on demand, which she wants.

In short, it must simply be said that, in morals, not only are the theories in doubt but also (and, in my view, more

[18] For an example of how this question of adequacy can be developed into a criticism of a utilitarianism, see my 'Act-Utilitarianism: Sidgwick or Bentham and Smart?', *Mind,* lxxxvi (1977), 95–101.

[19] R.M. Hare, 'A Critical Study of Rawls' "A Theory of Justice"', *Philosophical Quarterly,* 23 (1973), 144–55, 241–52.

[20] P. Singer, 'Sidgwick and Reflective Equilibrium', *The Monist,* lviii (1974), 490–517.

[21] J. Rawls, *A Theory of Justice* (Clarendon Press, Oxford, 1972). See, for example, pp. 20 ff., 48 ff.

importantly) even the test(s) of adequacy by which we might evaluate them; and to go on about moral rights under these conditions is not to argue the pertinent issues at all. Here, too, therefore, claims to rights do not play the serious and decisive role in morals which they play in Feinberg's paradigm, the law. For the quest for theses, standards, or principles of rightness, wrongness, and justification by which to ground, support, and justify claims to moral rights leads directly to a quest for agreed criteria of adequacy by which to adjudicate the conflicting normative ethics in which theses, standards, or principles find a home; and the derivation of these criteria remains a task, both crucial and fundamental, yet to be satisfactorily concluded. Thus, far from ever resolving anything in morals, claims to rights merely re-emphasize the unsatisfactory state in which the issues surrounding this question of adequacy remain; it is difficult, therefore, to see how these pertinent issues are or could be either argued or advanced by continually making such claims. Accordingly, until these issues are resolved, always assuming they can be, I do not see how it can be affirmed that women have a moral right to abortion on demand or that animals have a moral right to life.

To my mind, then, either moral rights are superfluous or we are not yet in a position to affirm that there are any; whichever it is, I cannot see that anything is lost by giving up claims to moral rights altogether. If such rights are superfluous, we do not require them in order to discuss our treatment of women or animals or the environment; and if there are not any, or it cannot be affirmed that there are, surely we would do better to concentrate directly on our treatment of women, animals, and the environment and upon the task of working out among us both principles of rightness and justification of treatment and criteria of adequacy for the assessment of the theories of which these principles will form a part?[22]

---

[22] I pursue the general line of argument in this chapter in my paper 'On Why We Would Do Better To Jettison Moral Rights', forthcoming.

II
Interests and
Rights

The transition from the major to the minor premiss of Nelson's argument can perhaps best be made by a consideration of H. J. McCloskey's position on animal interests and Tom Regan's criticism of it. For though I do not think McCloskey's way of tackling the claim that animals have interests a particularly fruitful one, and my own case against this claim neither follows nor relies upon his, an examination of Regan's arguments against McCloskey not only brings out some of the many issues swirling around the minor premiss but also introduces us to one of the favourite, most frequently used argument techniques of animal rightists, which I shall subsequently take up and comment upon.

In his paper 'Rights', McCloskey indicates his acceptance of the requirement that only beings which (can) have interests (can) have rights but goes on to deny that animals can have interests.[1] In his reply, 'McCloskey On Why Animals Cannot Have Rights',[2] Regan objects to this requirement in two ways: first, he queries whether it is in fact a requirement for the possession of rights; then, for the sake of argument, he concedes that it is and tries to show that animals can in fact satisfy it, which, if they can, establishes the truth of the Nelsonian minor premiss. On both counts, however, I find Regan's arguments lacking.

[1] *Philosophical Quarterly*, 15 (1965), 115–27. In recent years, McCloskey has done a good deal of work on rights; see, for example, 'The Right to Life', *Mind*, lxxxiv (1975), 403–25, and 'Human Needs, Rights and Political Values', *American Philosophical Quarterly*, 13 (1976), 1–11.
[2] T. Regan, 'McCloskey On Why Animals Cannot Have Rights', *Philosophical Quarterly*, 26 (1976), 251–7.

McCloskey does not think we can speak of what is *in* an animal's interests because such talk has an evaluative–prescriptive overtone. In the case of human beings, for example, what we mean when we say X is in A's interests is both that X will contribute to A's good or welfare – the evaluative component – and that A ought to care or be concerned about X – the prescriptive overtone. Since Regan takes it as common ground between himself and McCloskey that animals can have a good or a welfare, it must be the prescriptive overtone which McCloskey sticks at in the case of animals, and which Regan goes on to interpret in action-guiding terms, though such an interpretation is not essential to his purposes.

In order to question whether McCloskey's is in fact a requirement for the possession of rights, Regan tries to show that McCloskey is mistaken in thinking that talk of what is *in* a person's interests has or has invariably a prescriptive overtone. To do this, he produces the analogue to J. R. Searle's argument against Hare:[3] a prescriptive overtone cannot be an invariable feature of speaking of what is in a person's interests, since we can ask 'Is X in A's interests?' without issuing any prescription whatever, just as, Searle argues, we can ask 'Is X good?' without thereby commending X. Regan refers to Searle's attack but not to Hare's recent attempt at a rebuttal,[4] which dwells upon precisely the point that Regan is making. I shall not go into the matter here: I only stress that a defender of a McCloskey-like position, if he wishes to accept Regan's gambit of conducting the controversy in terms of meaning (see below), can fall back upon this rebuttal by Hare, in order to acquire grounds by which to defend the claim that we can only understand locutions of the form 'Is X in A's interests?' by first fully understanding (via an analysis of speech acts, assertion, mood, and sentence-frames) locutions of the form 'X is in A's interests', which possess, as Regan construes McCloskey, a prescriptive overtone.

Locutions of this latter form, however, give rise to a

---

[3] J.R. Searle, 'Meaning and Speech Acts', *Philosophical Review*, lxxi (1962), 423–32.

[4] R.M. Hare, 'Meaning and Speech Acts', *Philosophical Review*, lxxix (1970), 3–24.

different problem, according to Regan. If '*A* ought to do *X*' is part of the meaning of '*X* is in *A*'s interests', then we cannot cite the fact that *X* is in *A*'s interests as a *reason* for saying that '*A* ought to do *X*', since we shall already in part *mean* '*A* ought to do *X*'; and this is a mistake, for to cite the fact that *X* is in *A*'s interests is typically to provide *A* with a reason for doing *X* (and, we may add on Regan's behalf, for saying '*A* ought to do *X*'). This argument is objectionable on two counts, the second of which, if it can be sustained, undermines Regan's challenge to the legitimacy of McCloskey's requirement.

(1) The argument turns upon an implicit analysis of the relations between entailments and giving reasons, and it is easy to find cases which call this analysis into question, unless it is developed much more carefully. For example, if '*A* is a biped' is part of the meaning of '*A* is a man', then, according to Regan, we cannot cite the fact that *A* is a biped as a *reason* for saying '*A* is a man', since we shall already in part *mean* '*A* is a biped'. But this is false: the fact that *A* is a biped *is* a reason both for claiming and saying '*A* is a man', and we all treat it as such.

(2) The argument, and indeed the whole of Regan's challenge to the legitimacy of McCloskey's requirement, relies heavily upon his construing McCloskey as holding that a prescriptive overtone is *part of the meaning* of the expression '*X* is in *A*'s interests'.[5] Now whatever the rights and wrongs of this as an interpretation of McCloskey, a defender of a McCloskey-like position can escape the argument thus: he can argue that what he is claiming is not that there is a *prescriptive overtone to the meaning* of a phrase like '*X* is in *A*'s interests' but rather that there is a *prescriptive component in the analysis* of what it is to have interests. I am aware that this distinction is a controversial one, but there are some well-known, and, I think, currently received, applications of it. For example, according to Kant, 'This is an apple' does not have some utterly peculiar meaning, but his analysis of objects and what it is to be an object, just as much as Locke's analysis of material substance, is, at least to many,

⁵ 'McCloskey On Why Animals Cannot Have Rights', 255.

something very peculiar indeed. It is not the meaning of the word 'apple' but the analysis of what it is to be an object that turns upon the Copernican Revolution. Similarly, it is not the meaning of the sentence 'There is a table in the next room' but the analysis of the existence of unperceived tables that contemporary phenomenalists render in terms of counter-factual conditionals and that Mill and Russell hoped to render in terms of the permanent possibilities of sensations. Likewise, it is because of an analysis of, for example, rationality and of what it is *to be* rational that some people have thought that animals cannot have rights. So far as I can see, nothing compels one to say that '*A* ought to do *X*' is part of the meaning of '*X* is in *A*'s interests'.

What the defender of a McCloskey-like position is suggesting, then, is that the case of interests fits into this list of applications of the meaning/analysis distinction, so that he is free to formulate his position in terms of an analysis of what it is to have interests. And he holds that the analysis in question has two components, one evaluative, to the effect that *X* contributes or is thought to contribute to *A*'s good or welfare, the other prescriptive, to the effect that *A* ought to care or be concerned or prepared to do something about *X*. A position of this sort captures McCloskey's point without being open to Regan's objection.

But is it not open to an objection of a different sort? For it may be pointed out that the case of interests is not *exactly* like the other examples in the above list of applications of the meaning/analysis distinction, since it alone involves a change of mood between the analysandum and the analysans. This is certainly true, at least if we suppose that the prescriptive component to the analysans is rendered in the imperative mood; but I am not aware that, *per se*, this difference from the other examples is at all significant or amounts to an objection. It can be *turned into* an objection, of course, if it can be made part of some argument which yields as a conclusion that, for example, in an analysis of this sort, the analysans *cannot* be in a mood different from that of the analysandum. I do not know of any such argument, and the issue is much too peripheral to my concerns to be enlarged upon here; but, at the very least, an *a priori* claim of this sort is far too encompassing to be accepted without argument.

So far as the other side to Regan's attack on McCloskey's requirement is concerned, i.e. the claim that animals can indeed satisfy that requirement, and so have interests,[6] I think that the argument by which Regan supports this claim either yields an unwelcome result or, if it is to avoid this result, demands support of a kind very different from anything he has provided.

Regan suggests, on analogy with the cases of babies and the severely mentally-enfeebled, an analogy to which I shall return in the next chapter, that we can speak of what is *in* an animal's interests, in spite of the fact that the animal itself is not in a position to do anything about securing what is in its interests, just as we can speak of a blood transfusion's being in a baby's interests, in spite of the fact that the baby itself cannot see to having one. Thus, if there is a prescriptive (or action-guiding) overtone to 'It is in the baby's interests to have a blood transfusion', the prescription (or action-guidance) must apply not to the baby but to someone else, to, says Regan, 'some competent person who has it within his power to see that the baby gets what she needs'.[7] Likewise, if there is a prescriptive (or action-guiding) overtone to 'Treatment for worms is in Fido's interests', the prescription (or action-guidance) applies not to Fido, who does not see to his own treatment, but to 'some *other* competent being who has it within his power to see that Fido gets what he needs'.[8] In short, what is true in the case of the baby is true in the case of Fido; and both succeed or fail together in satisfying McCloskey's requirement.

Doubtless the most tempting reply to this argument is to observe that, eventually, the baby *will be* in a position to see to her treatment, whereas Fido *will never be* in a position to see about his complaint for worms. Presumably, however, Regan will object to this argument from potentiality, on the ground that it ignores the *present state* of the baby, which, in his own argument, appears to be a crucial consideration. We are not, therefore, to be allowed to invoke an argument

---

[6] I should add that Regan thinks animals can satisfy McCloskey's requirement whatever the outcome of his challenge to the legitimacy of that requirement.
[7] p. 257.   [8] p. 257 (italics in original).

from potentiality. And this fact, together with an implication of Regan's own argument, yields, I suggest, an unwelcome result.

The implication in question is this: though Regan switches from speaking of a 'competent person' seeing to the treatment of the baby to speaking of a 'competent being' seeing to the treatment of Fido, it is plain that a competent person is to see to Fido's treatment. The effect of Regan's argument, therefore, is to tie the existence of animal interests (and, hence, on McCloskey's requirement, animal rights) to the existence of human beings; for the unique feature of Regan's argument is that the prescriptive overtone to interest-ascriptions in the case of animals is directed at and applies to (competent) human beings, who are not themselves the possessors of those interests. Thus, if there are no people, animals do not have interests (nor, therefore, rights). Now because he treats the case of the baby as on all fours with the case of Fido, it follows on Regan's argument that, if there are no human beings other than the baby, if, in other words, there are no competent human beings, then the baby has no interests. And this is not commonly thought; that is, it is not commonly thought that a baby has interests only if there are other or competent human beings about. To take Regan's example, it would be quite peculiar to maintain that a blood transfusion is in baby Jane's interests *only if* there are other or competent human beings about. Doctors do not think that plenty of vitamin C is in Jane's interests only so long as there are people about to see that she receives some; rather, they think vitamin C in Jane's interests whether or not she ever receives any and, therefore, whether or not there are other people about to see that she does. Similarly, both doctors and we ourselves think the blood transfusion to be in Jane's interests whether or not there are other people about, competent or otherwise, to see to it; and one (but only one) of the reasons we think this is doubtless our implicit acceptance of something like what I have above called the argument from potentiality, to which Regan, however, will not allow us to appeal. Without such an appeal, Regan's argument yields an unwelcome result; but with such an appeal, we acquire a ground for treating the case of Jane differently from that of Fido, and the basis of Regan's argument — that the cases of Jane and Fido are on all fours — is thereby undermined.

There are two likely paths of resistance here. One is to argue that, though Regan's position ties the existence of animal interests and the interests of babies to the existence of human beings, it does not require the present existence of human beings. Rather, a device common to 'desert-island' problems may be employed: this is to argue that, in respect of the case at hand, the mode of discourse involving concepts such as interests and rights would not have developed except among human beings who were, so to speak, interest-recognizers and competent interest-pursuers. In this way, one might try to sustain a link between interests and the existence of other or competent human beings even should a situation arise in which there are no, or no competent, human beings except baby Jane.

Regan's problem, I think, is to make this kind of defence sit well with the argument of his paper. He contends that animals can satisfy McCloskey's requirement and provides an argument to this end. What is the unique feature of this argument? It is that the prescriptive overtone of interest-ascriptions in the cases of animals and babies is *directed at* and *applies to* (competent) human beings, who are not themselves the possessors of those interests. Now just as we can use prescriptive language without actually prescribing, so we might be able to use interest-language without actually addressing specific interest-recognizers and interest-pursuers; but what we cannot do on Regan's position, if we interpret talk of having interests in the light of McCloskey's requirement, as does Regan for the purpose at hand, is to use prescriptive language without *addressing somebody or other*, to use prescriptive language and *address no one at all*. For the unique feature of Regan's argument — that the prescriptive overtone to interest-ascriptions in the cases of animals and babies is *directed at* and *applies to* human beings — would thereby have been sacrificed. These human beings in the case of Jane need not be specific individuals, such as her parents, but Regan's position does not allow that the prescriptive overtone in question be addressed to no human being whatever. Accordingly, there seem three possibilites. First, the prescriptive overtone is addressed to presently existing people. I have already argued that the effect of this position is to tie the existence of interests in the case of baby Jane to the existence of other or competent human beings and that this is implausible. Second, the prescriptive overtone is addressed to previously existing people. Quite independently of questions of logical propriety, this position seems implausible also, since, presumably, in no case could dead people now act upon a prescription in respect of baby Jane's blood transfusion, so that such a prescription would be wholly pointless, if thought to be addressed to them. Third, the prescriptive overtone is addressed to people who will exist. Though this position avoids the problems of the previous one, it, too, seems implausible. For is it plausible to maintain that a blood transfusion is now in baby Jane's interests — otherwise, not — only if there are going to be future people to see that she receives one?[9] At the very least, it would be peculiar to hold that doctors could not properly decide whether plenty of vitamin C was in Jane's interests until they could first determine whether or not there were going to be future people.

A second path of resistance is, despite appearances, to deny that Regan's position ties the existence of animal interests and the interests of babies to the existence of human beings and to make it out rather to be about the meaning of such sentences as 'It is in baby Jane's interests to have a blood transfusion' when there are no or no competent human beings about. This, I take it, is what Regan does in a subsequent paper.[10] Very briefly, Regan's point now is this: the sentence 'It is in baby Jane's interests to have a blood transfusion' only has a prescriptive meaning if there is some competent human being about to see that she receives one; if there is no such human being about, or no human beings whatever about, then, though the blood transfusion remains in her interests, the sentence 'It is in baby Jane's interests to have a blood transfusion' no longer has a prescriptive meaning.

[9] One bizarre feature of thinking this plausible is that the complaint which requires Jane to have the blood transfusion in the first place could steadily worsen, yet, because it became increasingly clear (for whatever reason) that there were to be no future people, the transfusion would cease to be in her interests.

[10] T. Regan, 'Frey on Interests and Animal Rights', *Philosophical Quarterly*, 27 (1977), 335-7.

Thus, if we assume with McCloskey (as Regan does, for the sake of argument) that interest-talk has a prescriptive overtone or meaning, then Regan contends that speaking of what is in a baby's or an animal's interests loses its prescriptive meaning (or can have no prescriptive meaning) unless there are competent human beings about to see that the baby or the animal receives what is in its interests.

This is Regan's claim. But if we seek for the argument by which he supports it, we come up empty-handed. This is puzzling, since the claim is not presented as the guarantor of its own truth; it is more puzzling still, since the general position of which it appears to be an instance — that prescriptions cease to have prescriptive meaning when the question of compliance ceases in the circumstances to arise — is, if true at all, by no means *obviously* true. I mean, how does it follow from the fact that a prescription cannot in the circumstances be complied with that the prescription has no prescriptive meaning? If ten people are chained to the floor and someone comes in and says 'Get up off the floor!', I should prefer to say that the prescription in these circumstances cannot be complied with, even if the ten are otherwise willing, not that this sentence has no *meaning*, has no prescriptive meaning. At least in part, the prescriptive meaning of such sentences is a function of the sentence-frame type, the mood of the sentence, the meanings of the constituent words, and the general characteristics of imperatival sentences in English, none of which, it seems to me, are of necessity bound to alter simply because compliance is not open in the circumstances.

Furthermore, there is an important distinction to be drawn here, which I can best bring out by adapting an example Ryle once used in a lecture.[11] Suppose in the middle of a vast jungle, nailed to a large tree, is a sign which says 'No cars are to be parked within fifty feet of this sign': I want to say this sign is meaningful but pointless. It is meaningful, as is evidenced by the fact that we understand it, which in turn explains why we laugh upon reading it. It is, however, pointless, since the possibility of complying or not complying with it does not arise in the circumstances (no people, no cars, middle of the jungle). Now in understanding this sentence, what we

---

[11] My discussion of this distinction also owes a debt to R.M. Hare.

understand, I suggest, is not merely that the words mean such and such but also that the sentence, in English and in the imperative, prescribes the parking of cars more than fifty feet from the sign. We understand the sentence, that is, as an imperative, as having prescriptive meaning, whether or not there are or have been cars parked more than fifty feet from the sign. Because there are no people and no cars in the middle of the jungle, however, there is no point to such a prescription. But to say that the prescription is pointless is not to say that it is not a prescription; it is in the present instance to say only that compliance with it does not arise in the circumstances. If someone wants to claim that, these features notwithstanding, this English sentence in the imperative loses its prescriptive meaning when it crops up like this in the jungle, then I think we are owed an argument which establishes that this is so and therein an explanation which recounts just why it is so. Otherwise, why should we not say in Regan's case precisely the same as in this one, that the sentence 'It is in baby Jane's interests to have a blood transfusion' is meaningful but pointless, in conditions where there are no competent people about to see that Jane receives the transfusion?

It is, in short, at least arguable that sentences can retain their prescriptive meaning, and so remain prescriptions, in spite of the fact that there are no competent people about, so that, since Regan's claim that sentences lose their prescriptive meaning under such a condition is not the guarantor of its own truth, and since the more general position to which it would seem to belong — that prescriptions cease to have prescriptive meaning when the question of compliance ceases in the circumstances to arise — is at least dubious, we require some argument to show that his claim *is* true.

I conclude, therefore, that Regan's argument to show that animals satisfy McCloskey's requirement either yields an unwelcome result or, in order to avoid this result, requires support of a kind quite beyond anything he provides. Whichever it is, animals have not been shown to have interests, with the result that the minor premiss in the Nelsonian argument for animal rights is not established. The main and more powerful cases to establish the truth of this premiss, however, are yet to come.

III

The Argument from Marginal Cases

In the last chapter we touched upon one of the favourite, most frequently used argument techniques of animal rightists, and a few words on this technique are necessary.[1] The technique consists in using the cases of babies and the severely mentally-enfeebled in order to try to force the inclusion of animals within the class of right-holders.

Those who use this technique proceed as follows: they take a criterion for the possession of moral rights suggested by philosophers and others and show that it excludes babies and the severely mentally-enfeebled from the class of right-holders; since babies and the severely mentally-enfeebled do have rights, this criterion must be rejected as a criterion for the possession of rights. Thus, the technique gives rise to an argument, which might be called the argument from marginal cases:[2]

(1) Criterion X, while excluding animals, also excludes babies and the severely mentally-enfeebled from the class of right-holders;

(2) Babies and the severely mentally-enfeebled, however, do have rights and so fall within this class;

---

[1] In 'Animal Rights', *Canadian Journal of Philosophy*, vii (1977), 161–78, Jan Narveson also criticizes the argument from marginal cases. I am largely in agreement with Narveson's criticisms, though they are different from my own. For a reply to Narveson, see T. Regan, 'Narveson on Egoism and the Rights of Animals', *Canadian Journal of Philosophy*, vii (1977), 179–86, in which Regan comes out once again in support of the argument. See also Rodman, 'The Liberation of Nature?', 88 f.

[2] I follow Narveson in so labelling it (op. cit. 167).

(3) Therefore, criterion X must be rejected as a criterion for the possession of rights.

Obviously, this argument is essentially negative and indirect, in that it does not seek to establish that animals *have* rights but rather to undermine criteria the application of which yield the result that they do not have rights. (Of course, the hope, if not implication, is that, if we go on to adopt a criterion for the possession of rights that *includes* babies and the severely mentally-enfeebled within the class of right-holders, then it will also include animals within this class.) For example, rationality as a criterion must be discarded, for otherwise we obtain a singularly objectionable result:

If we accord moral rights on the basis of rationality, what of the status of newly born children, "low grade" mental patients, "intellectual cabbages", and so on? Logically, accepting this criterion, they must have no, or diminished, moral rights.[3]

And what of a criterion of accepting and discharging moral duties and obligations?

Secondly, and I think this objection is persuasive in showing the difficult consequences of the argument, there are some human beings quite incapable of moral duties — for instance "low grade" mental patients. By logical inference, accepting the validity of the argument, we would be committed to the view that they also possess no moral rights.[4]

The argument from marginal cases is found throughout the literature on animal rights, and by its means such widely different criteria as the possession of rationality or of language, the ability to make choices or to exercise a free will, the recognition and discharge of moral obligations, the possession of a culture, the acceptance of and participation within societal and communal relationships, the possession of interests in McCloskey's sense (where this connotes that S is in one's own welfare, that one cares or exhibits concern about S, and that one is prepared to do something about and perhaps even to think that one ought to do something about S), etc. are all allegedly undermined as criteria for the possession of rights.

[3] A. Linzey, *Animal Rights* (S.P.C.K., London, 1976), p. 24.
[4] Ibid. 23–4.

In fact, it is the argument from marginal cases which is suspect, or so I suggest. It hinges upon premiss (2), that is, upon treating the cases of babies and the severely mentally-enfeebled as open and shut so far as the possession of rights is concerned. Premiss (2), however, is not obvious but requires defence. For unless it can be defended, opponents of animal rights will argue that, if babies and the severely mentally-enfeebled do not have rights, then there is *per se* no reason to reject an animal-excluding criterion which also excludes babies and the severely mentally-enfeebled from the class of right-holders. Put differently, proponents of animal rights are free to use any defence of premiss (2) which is consistent with their position; but they must have *some defence or other* of premiss (2) if, for example, the animal-excluding criterion of the possession of a culture is to be undermined or rendered suspect *on the ground* that it excludes babies and the severely mentally-enfeebled from the class of right-holders.

But is it so very clear that babies and the severely mentally-enfeebled do have rights — do have rights, that is, and this is the point, without the addition of *further arguments* which themselves exclude animals as right-holders?[5]

For example, consider again the rationality requirement:

Only beings which are rational possess rights.

Given a suitably restrictive analysis of rationality, babies and the severely mentally-enfeebled will be excluded from the class of rational beings and so from the class of right-holders; on this requirement, they simply have no rights. Since, upon the same restrictive analysis of rationality, animals also are not rational, it follows that they have no rights either. The position I have in mind here is a radical one, at least to this extent, that it excludes not only all animals but also some and perhaps even a good many humans from the class of right-holders.

Now three traditional arguments by which it has been thought that babies and the severely mentally-enfeebled can

---

[5] I remind the reader that, in order to meet and confound animal rightists on their own ground, I assume with them, except in Ch. I, and, eventually, in the Postscript, that there are moral rights.

be included within the class of right-holders and that premiss (2) can be defended all specifically exclude Fido from this class.

(1) One might try to include the baby, as we saw in the last chapter, by means of the *potentiality argument*: the baby is potentially rational. Of course, the baby is not at present rational, and if actual rationality is insisted upon, then the baby has no rights. On the other hand, the potentiality argument does separate the case of the baby from that of Fido, who is not conceded even potential rationality.

To the claim that, in some sense of 'rational', some infant animals are potentially rational,[6] I draw attention to the fact that the rationality criterion for right-possession is prefaced with the restriction 'given a suitably restrictive analysis of rationality'. This restriction, obviously, invites the retort that, if rigorously applied, it will exclude from the class of right-holders not only animals but also, for example, babies and the severely mentally-enfeebled, a result which the restriction's proponent, however, is quite prepared to accept.

(2) One might try to include the severely mentally-enfeebled by means of the *similarity argument*: in all respects apart from rationality and perhaps certain mental accomplishments, the severely mentally-enfeebled betray strong physical similarities in their appearance to the remainder of our species, and it would and does offend our species horribly to deprive such similar creatures of rights. If this argument is rejected, on the ground that rationality is the requirement for possessing rights and other similarities are beside the point, then the severely mentally-enfeebled do not have rights. On the other hand, the similarity argument does separate the severely mentally-enfeebled from Fido, who does not bear anything like sufficient physical similarities to ourselves to warrant similar inclusion.[7]

[6] Cf. D. Jamieson, T. Regan, 'Animal Rights: A Reply to Frey', *Analysis*, 38 (1978), 32–6. In his *Thinking Animals: Animals and the Development of Human Intelligence* (Viking Press, New York, 1978), Paul Shepard claims that not only the ways in which we see ourselves but also the full development of our minds depends upon the survival of animals, a claim which, even if true, does not *show* that animals are rational or rational in the appropriate sense or to the appropriate degree.

[7] Jamieson and Regan (p. 35) contend that cases will arise in which some

Animal liberationists, of course, will also object to the similarity argument on the ground that is smacks strongly of speciesism. For it does enshrine the active discrimination against other species in favour of our own, a form of discrimination nearly all of us practise. If an unknown dog and an unknown man are drowning, and we can only save one, nearly all of us will seek to save the man, a fact which reflects the value we actually do place, whether wisely or not, upon their relative lives.

(3) One might try to include both babies and the severely mentally-enfeebled by means of the *religious argument*: babies and the severely mentally-enfeebled possess immortal souls. If this argument is rejected, on the ground that, even if they possess immortal souls, beings must also possess rationality in order to have rights, or on the ground that there is no good evidence for the existence of such souls, then neither babies nor the severely mentally-enfeebled possess rights. On the other hand, the religious argument does separate both from Fido, who is not conceded an immortal soul by the argument's proponents.

The upshot is this. Unless one of these arguments is accepted, we have no basis upon which to differentiate the cases of babies and the severely mentally-enfeebled from that of animals; and if all of these arguments *are rejected*, and there are, I want to stress, serious objections to each, then it follows on the requirement under consideration that babies, the severely mentally-enfeebled, and animals are alike in not being right-holders. In other words, these traditional defences of premiss (2) collapse, with the result that the premiss cannot sustain the weight put upon it. If, however, one of these arguments *is accepted*, so that babies and the severely mentally-enfeebled are held to fall within the class of right-

---

animals betray stronger similarities in their appearance to the rest of us than do some of those whom they dub 'non-paradigmatic humans'. To this, I can only observe that I have never seen the dog, cat, monkey, bird, or fish that more strongly resembled us than did a former colleague's baby daughter, who was both severely deformed (through her mother's use of thalidomide) and mentally retarded, or a friend's husband, who suffered first-degree burns over more than fifty per cent of his body. Nor am I aware of any reason why I should think I *will meet* the dog, cat, monkey, bird, or fish that more strongly resembles the rest of us than does my former colleague's baby daughter.

holders, then we find that this argument itself specifically *excludes* animals from this class. In other words, premiss (1) is false, since the particular animal-excluding criterion for the possession of rights in question *does not exclude* babies and the severely mentally-enfeebled. In respect of these traditional defences of premiss (2), therefore, either premiss (2) is not established or premiss (1) is false.

Premiss (2), then, is in doubt: it is simply not clear that babies and the severely mentally-enfeebled do have moral rights, with the result that the argument from marginal cases, by which the animal rightist hopes to force the inclusion of animals within the class of right-holders, is itself plainly suspect.

It is at this point that an appeal to sentiency, to which I shall return off and on throughout the remainder of this book, will doubtless be made, in the hope of finding a defence of premiss (2) which not only manages to squeeze babies and the severely mentally-enfeebled but also most animals into the class of right-holders.[8]

My initial difficulties with the appeal to sentiency are those which are raised every time this appeal is discussed. First, *merely citing* sentiency as a criterion for the possession of moral rights neither shows that it is one nor even creates a presumption that it is, and until some arguments in these respects are provided, it is not apparent how merely appealing to sentiency is supposed *to show* that babies and the severely mentally-enfeebled do have rights. As we shall see in subsequent chapters, such arguments are scarce on the ground. Second, any argument to show or to create a presumption that sentiency is a criterion for the possession of moral rights must *at the very least* involve both attaching some specific meaning to that term and, what is equally important, going on to explore critically the implications this meaning has for the class of right-holders. Once this is done, certain objectionable implications may well be seen to result.

The term 'sentiency' can be and has been used to mean a number of things. For the sake of brevity, I shall indicate but four things it may be taken to mean, together with a few of

<hr>

[8] Jamieson and Regan (p. 36) make such an appeal.

the implications these meanings have for the class of right-holders.

(1) If 'sentiency' is taken to mean 'reaction to stimuli', then a sentiency criterion compels us to concede rights to, for example, certain plants and perhaps even litmus paper; and it has not usually been thought that these things are even candidates for having rights.[9]

(2) If 'sentiency' is taken to mean 'reaction to sensory stimuli', then a sentiency criterion compels us to concede rights, for example, to even some of the 'lowest' forms of animal life, forms which even proponents of animal rights, who nearly always dwell upon the 'higher' animals, usually ignore. I am not claiming that mosquitoes, flies, and ants do not have rights, only that most people almost certainly need convincing that they do.

(3) If 'sentiency' is taken to mean the 'capacity to feel pain', so that only beings which can feel pain have rights, then a sentiency criterion yields three immediate results. First, it compels us to exclude from the class of right-holders, for example, foetuses, individuals suffering certain types of nervous damage, and the comatose, exclusions which are doubtless going to be objectionable to many people. (This upshot, rather interestingly, has provoked some strange theses in reply. To take only the comatose, Mary Ann Warren would have us believe that the comatose have a capacity to feel pain which just happens to be inoperative.[10] Presumably, therefore, the irreversibly comatose have a capacity to feel pain which it just happens *cannot* become operative. But unless talk of their capacity in this regard means merely that

[9] The cases of plants and trees have recently been taken up by environmentalists and others, and the claim that trees and forests have moral rights is now sometimes to be met with. I shall have occasion to return to this claim several times in remaining chapters, though I might refer the reader forward (Ch. XI, n. 30) for a word of caution on the use to which I put this claim in Chapters IV and XI. Also, in discussing reaction to stimuli, we must not overlook Leonard Nelson's most unusual case of the electric bell (see Ch. V, n. 5), which responds to stimuli, according to him, but which no one will think has rights.

[10] Mary Ann Warren, 'Do Potential People Have Moral Rights?', *Canadian Journal of Philosophy*, vii (1977), 284. There is the question, of course, of quite how to define 'irreversible coma'; on this, see H.K. Beecher, 'After the "Definition of Irreversible Coma"', *New England Journal of Medicine*, 281 (1969), 1070-1.

their nervous system remains intact, which possibility I consider below, I do not know what it means to speak of having capacities which are incapable of being exercised. Regan, on the other hand, has at one time urged that comatose human beings are not human beings.[11] Presumably, therefore, when I slip into the room of Smith, who is irreversibly comatose, and stab him through the heart, whatever else I may be guilty of, appearances notwithstanding, I cannot be guilty of murder, assault, etc.) Second, a sentiency criterion on the present interpretation compels us, at the same time as excluding foetuses, those with certain types of nervous damage, and the comatose, to include within the class of right-holders, for example, lizards, frogs, and, if a recent television programme is to be believed, shrimps and lobsters. I am not claiming that lizards, frogs, shrimps, and lobsters do not have rights, only that, once again, most people almost certainly need convincing that they do, especially when it is alleged that foetuses, those suffering nervous damage, the comatose, human 'vegetables', the 'brain dead', etc. do not. Third, an individual has rights on this construal of a sentiency criterion up to the moment, for example, when he lapses into a coma and can no longer feel pain, at which time his rights go out of existence; should he later emerge from the coma, however, his rights presumably pop back into existence again, the moment he can feel pain. Surely a view of this sort needs argument? For, on the face of it, is it plausible to suggest, for example, that the right many have wanted to claim for human beings to be treated as an end and not as a means pops in and out of existence like this? After all,

---

[11] T. Regan, 'The Moral Basis of Vegetarianism', *Canadian Journal of Philosophy*, v (1975), 193. In conversation, Regan has told me that he no longer holds this view. I give it here only to indicate how appeals to sentiency, once the term is given some specific meaning and that meaning is explored, can yield difficulties.

   One might argue here, of course, that there is a question about whether the irreversibly comatose are alive or dead; see, for example, J.R. Harp, 'Criteria for the Determination of Death', *Anesthesiology*, 40 (1974), 391–7, and P.D.G. Skegg, 'Irreversibly Comatose Individuals: "Alive" or "Dead"?', *Cambridge Law Journal*, 33 (1974), 130–44. This question, however, is still only raised hypothetically and in the interest of promulgating competing definitions of death; for it remains true in Anglo-American law that the irreversibly comatose can be murdered, which I presume would be impossible unless the law still regarded the individuals in question as alive. For some competing definitions of death, see P. M. Black, 'Three Definitions of Death', *The Monist*, lx (1977), 136–46.

what has the dignity and respect of my being an end in itself
to do with my ability to feel pain? Proponents of this particular right are certainly not going to regard the comatose,
because they cannot feel pain, as ceasing to be ends in themselves, so that the treatment we mete out to them is not
something we have morally to trouble ourselves about. (I
return to the examples of this section in subsequent chapters.)

(4) If 'sentiency' is taken to mean the 'possession of a
nervous system remarkably similar to our own',[12] then a
sentiency criterion compels us to deny rights not only to
many animals and creatures of the sea, which animal rightists
themselves may be reluctant to do, but also to those people
who will follow us but who do not as yet exist. Increasingly,
more and more people are coming to think that future people
do have rights. Thus, a good deal of the present concern with
and writing on ecology is premissed on the fact that future
beings, who do not now have a nervous system at all (and,
come to that, do not feel pain), nevertheless have moral
rights in respect of the environment. Increasingly, too, reasons are being advanced as to why the law ought to concern
itself with the protection of these rights. I am not claiming
that future people do have moral rights, only that most
writers and thinkers on the subject do not think the question of whether they do has anything to do with the type of
nervous system they have or with the possession of a nervous
system at all, any more than they think that the question
of whether a foetus has rights is a matter of finding out something about the physical nature of its nervous system.

The point, then, is not that these implications of the
various construals of a sentiency criterion cannot be embraced or tolerated, but that, once 'sentiency' is given a
meaning and once the implications of this meaning for the
class of right-holders is explored, certain objectionable results, objectionable, in any event, to a good many people,
become apparent. And if a sentiency criterion is suspect,
then its use to substantiate premiss (2) of the argument from
marginal cases is suspect. In short, it remains unclear that

---

[12] Cf. Singer, *Animal Liberation*, pp. 12 f., 185 f.

premiss (2) is true, which in turn means, as we have seen, that the use of the argument from marginal cases to try to force the inclusion of animals within the class of right-holders is itself of doubtful success. We are by no means finished with a sentiency criterion, however, and ultimate judgement upon it must be deferred.

IV

Mental States and Moral Standing

Strange as it may seem, in view of their well-known avoidance of, if not antipathy towards, moral rights, the use of pain as a criterion for the possession of such rights owes a debt to act-utilitarians. I do not refer to the fact that Regan, Clark, Singer, and virtually all other animal rightists and/or liberationists quote such utilitarians with approval on the necessity of paying attention to the fact that cats and dogs can suffer; rather, I refer to the role suffering plays in the act-utilitarian's general conception of morality. Though this role is a well known and much discussed one in utilitarian theory, a few words on it here, and its eventual linkage to the issue of moral rights, may not be out of place.

According to act-utilitarianism, an act is right if and only if its consequences are at least as good as those of any alternative. This general characterization of a type of normative ethical theory can be qualified in several respects in order to produce different though related versions of the theory. One way it can be qualified, perhaps the best-known way, is by employing different standards of goodness, at least one of which must be a feature of any act-utilitarianism, since an act is right only if its consequences are as *good* as those of any alternative. It is customary to distinguish between hedonistic and non-hedonistic or ideal standards; Bentham's hedonism, Mill's distinction between qualities of pleasure, Sidgwick's addition of a principle of justice independent of his hedonism, Stace's emphasis upon happiness and not pleasure, and Rashdall's and Moore's claim that there are a number of things other than pleasure and/or happiness which are good-in-themselves are all exceedingly familiar, however, and I shall not bother to develop them. Whatever standard of goodness is adopted will be a standard of intrinsic goodness: Bentham's view is that only pleasure is good-in-itself, Stace's, that only happiness is good-in-itself, Moore's, that there are a number of things good-in-themselves. Moreover, though there has been a recent change by some act-utilitarians, as we shall see below and in Chapter X, those things good-in-themselves have traditionally been considered to be certain mental states, grouped together and called 'pleasure', 'happiness', etc.

It is obvious that the act-utilitarian's account of rightness is partially grounded in and turns upon his view of goodness, and his account of goodness, at least traditionally, is grounded in and turns upon the view that only mental states are good-in-themselves. The determination of right and wrong, therefore, is a function of pleasurable and painful mental states, and the exact determination is made according to which states predominate over the other. Thus, when Bentham speaks of right and wrong as 'fastened to [the] throne' of pleasure and pain,[1] he means that right and wrong are tied to these states of mind. He and the other early utilitarians did, of course, as Quinton has noted,[2] treat these mental states as cognitive states as well, but this need not detain us. For the important point here is *that* suffering has been tied to mental states and *that* it is the presence of such states to which right and wrong are 'fastened'.

How minimal a view of 'mental state' should we adopt? This, too, we need not agonize over. For it has been an article of faith among all act-utilitarians, past and present, that cats and dogs can be in the mental states necessary for them to suffer; and though I myself think that this means merely that they can suffer unpleasant sensations (see chapters VIII and XI), there is sufficient backing for the view that having sensations is having (certain) mental states to

---

[1] *Introduction to the Principles of Morals and Legislation,* ed. J. Harrison (Blackwell, Oxford, 1948), Ch. I, section 1.
[2] *Utilitarian Ethics* (Macmillan, London, 1973), p. 5.

enable this to pass without further critical comment. Bernard
Williams captures the point nicely:

> Traditionally utilitarians have tended to regard happiness or, again,
> pleasure, as experiences or sensations which were related to actions and
> activity as effect to cause; and, granted that view, utilitarianism will in-
> deed see the value of all action as derivative, intrinsic value being re-
> served for the experiences of happiness.[3]

Williams goes on to caution us, however, against becoming
so pre-occupied with this view that we cannot see its limit-
ation, which consists in tying the discussion of utilitarianism
'to inadequate conceptions of happiness or pleasure',[4] that
is, in precluding actions and activities themselves, as opposed
to experiences and sensations, 'from having intrinsic value'.[5]
Some modern act-utilitarians want to broaden the class of the
intrinsically valuable to include actions and activities chosen
for their own sake, and Williams allows that 'we must be able
to recognize as versions of utilitarianism those which. . .take
as central some notion such as *satisfaction*, and connect that
criterially with such matters as the activities which a man will
freely choose to engage in'.[6] Williams's cautionary note
amounts to this: we must not adhere so rigidly to the minimal
view of what has intrinsic value that we fail to recognize as
utilitarians those very recent theorists who want to include
certain actions and activities among the intrinsically valuable.
It is in the light of this cautionary note that Williams identifies as the central theme of consequentialist/act-utilitarian
ethics that 'the only kind of thing that has intrinsic value is
states of affairs, and that anything else that has value has it
because it conduces to some intrinsically valuable state of
affairs'.[7] We need not trouble with the phrase 'state of affairs'
here, since it is broader than 'experiences or sensations' in
order to take account of Williams's note about recent utilitarian theorists; the important point is that the minimal view
of intrinsic value has not been repudiated, but merely supple-
mented, and there are still numerous act-utilitarians who
prefer the mental state view.

---

[3] *A Critique of Utilitarianism*, in J.J.C. Smart, B. Williams, *Utilitarianism:
For and Against* (Cambridge University Press, Cambridge, 1973), p. 84.
[4] Ibid. 85.   [5] Ibid. 86.
[6] Ibid. 85; italics in original.   [7] Ibid. 83.

With suffering tied to mental states; with animals allowed to be in such states; with these states being the ultimate ground of right and wrong and, bearing in mind Williams's cautionary note, the only things possessed of intrinsic value; and with everything else having value only if 'it conduces to some intrinsically valuable' state of mind; it is clear that the vast bulk of animals are covered by utilitarian calculations of right and wrong. Put differently, it is the mental state view of suffering and the mental state view of value which enable the majority of animals to be encompassed by this utilitarian moral outlook, not some theological view which lays down that we are all creatures of God or some evolutionary–ethological stricture which stresses our common animal heritage and endowment.

It should be obvious why animal rightists (or, indeed, advocates of moral rights in general) will be attracted by this utilitarian picture. By grounding moral rights in the having of the mental states necessary in order to suffer, which, on the minimal interpretation, is the having of pleasurable and painful 'experiences or sensations', the argument for the possession of these rights by animals becomes relatively straightforward. For there is nothing a cat need *do* — no test to meet to demonstrate its intelligence, no test to meet to demonstrate its rationality, no set of actions it must perform to demonstrate its autonomy, no sounds or gestures it must make to demonstrate its command of language — in order to suffer. It need only continue to exist. Even to non-act-utilitarians, then, the mental state view of suffering and the mental state view of value which underlies it can appear attractive.

On the other hand, this view of value does give rise to an obvious difficulty, namely, that anything which cannot have mental states cannot be possessed of intrinsic value. Writing of utilitarianism, Stuart Hampshire puts the point thus:

. . . nothing else counts but the states of mind, and perhaps, more narrowly, the states of feeling, of persons; or, more generously, in Bentham and G.E. Moore, of sentient creatures. Anything else that one might consider, in the indefinite range of natural and man-made things, is to be reckoned as mere machinery, as only a possible instrument for producing the all-important — literally all-important — states of feeling. From this moral standpoint, the whole machinery of the natural order, other than states of mind, just is machinery, useful or harmful in proportion as it promotes or prevents desired states of feeling.[8]

The implications of this difficulty are well-recognized in utilitarian theory, and utilitarians have moved to meet it;[9] but the implications of this difficulty for animal rightists and their use of suffering in order to confer moral rights upon animals have been little discussed,[10] and they are very much worth noting. So let us look at these issues again, this time with animal rightists (and/or liberationists) in mind.

Since nearly all animal rightists are very keen to include under the term 'sentient' the 'capacity to experience pain',[11] we do well to remind ourselves that the dictionary meaning of this term is 'having the power of sense-perception'. For we must not get things in reverse: the 'higher' animals are not sentient because they can have experiences of pain; rather, they can have experiences of pain because they possess senses and are sentient proper, i.e. because they have the power of sense-perception. No creature which lacks the power of sense-perception can experience pain, indeed, in the appropriate sense for our purposes here, can have experiences or mental states at all. Since almost no one today denies that at least the 'higher' animals can, because they are sentient proper, suffer, it follows on this usage that they are sentient; and if we assume the truth of a sentiency criterion for the possession of moral rights, it follows that they have such rights.

To this basic account of sentiency, one or two animal rightists want to make the odd addition. Joel Feinberg, for example, wants to include under the term 'sentience' the various elements which make up a conative life, such as wishes and desires, which he thinks the 'higher' animals have.[12] (I consider the important issue of whether animals

[8] *Morality and Pessimism* (Cambridge University Press, Cambridge, 1972), p. 3.

[9] See, for example, James Griffin's 'Are There Incommensurable Values?', *Philosophy and Public Affairs*, 7 (1977), 39–59.

[10] The only discussion I am aware of is John Rodman's in 'The Liberation of Nature?', 88–93. My discussion here owes a debt to these pages in Rodman, though I do not wish to imply that he or any other environmentalist would share my position on moral rights generally or on animal rights in particular.

[11] See, for example, A. Linzey, *Animal Rights*, Ch. 3.

[12] 'The Rights of Animals and Unborn Generations', 49–51. See also Rodman, op. cit. 89.

can have desires in Chapters VI, VII, and VIII.)

Now I think what is common to all of these items included under the term 'sentience' — to sense-perceptions, suffering, and the elements of a conative life — is, roughly speaking, that they either are or presuppose experiences or mental states; and experiences or mental states, clearly, are phenomena which are *had* by creatures. Creatures which have or can have them are sentient and are generally labelled 'beings'; creatures which cannot have them are not sentient and are not generally labelled 'beings' but 'things'. Notice two points. First, a being is not sentient because it has or can have this or that *kind* of experiences — as if having experiences of this or that kind *constituted* sentiency — but rather because it has or can have experiences or mental states *per se*. The point may be put in the form of an example. Suppose an operation were performed on a rabbit as the result of which, *ex hypothesi*, though the rabbit could no longer feel pleasure or pain, its other experiences or states were unaffected: would not the rabbit nevertheless remain a sentient being? For it still eats, sleeps, hops about, chases other rabbits, etc. Second, Mary Ann Warren's point about whether a being who has or can have experiences *prefers* some kinds of experiences to others, for example, pleasurable to painful ones, is a secondary affair; for only if the creature has or can have experiences or mental states in the first place do questions of its preferring some kinds to others arise.[13]

On a sentiency criterion, then, I agree with John Rodman (and Mary Ann Warren) that it is ultimately the fact that human beings and the 'higher' animals have experiences or mental states which is used to distinguish them from everything else and is the ultimate and fundamental basis of the claim that they are the possessors of moral rights. Thus, it is because trees and shrubs do not and/or cannot have experiences or mental states, not because they do not and/or cannot have experiences or states of a particular kind and not because they do not and/or cannot prefer one kind of experiences or states to another, that they are not sentient beings. And, lacking sentiency, they have no rights.

---

[13] I disagree, therefore, with this part of Mary Ann Warren's account of sentiency; see 'Do Potential People Have Moral Rights?', 283-6.

It is ironic, to say the least, that this result of the application of a sentiency criterion, in large measure in order to combat discrimination (against the 'higher' animals), is itself, as Rodman has noted,[14] blatantly discriminatory in character. For, to put the matter rather pompously, it condemns the whole of non-sentient creation, including the 'lower' animals, at best to a much inferior moral status or, as we shall see, at worst to a status completely outside morality. In essence, non-sentient creation is 'simply there' for sentient creation to do with as it sees fit. Animal rightists and animal liberationists in general have often objected to the Christian view of man as having dominion over the rest of creation;[15] but the only revolution they effect by means of an appeal to a mental state of view of value is to give man and the 'higher' animals dominion over the rest of creation. The criterion of sentiency, then, does not eliminate discrimination; on the contrary, it broadens the category of those who can practise it, or, in the case of the 'higher' animals, who can have it practised on their behalf. If one is going to complain about this sort of thing in the first place, why go on to practise it by means of a sentiency criterion?[16] (I return to this question in Chapter XI.)

Any animal rightist who insists upon the adoption of a sentiency criterion for the possession of moral rights is almost certainly going to lose the support of a good many environmentalists, and it is not surprising that the animal and environmental lobbies in the United States have come into conflict. For unless environmentalists rather implausibly seek

---

[14] See Rodman, op. cit. 91.

[15] A. Linzey, op. cit., Ch. 2; P. Singer, *Animal Liberation,* Ch. 5; S.R.L. Clark, *The Moral Status of Animals,* Chs. II, V, and VIII. For Clark's views on nature and the environment, which are especially relevant to my concerns in this chapter, see particularly pp. 158 ff. Of interest here also is J. Black's *The Dominion of Man: The Search for Ecological Responsibility* (Edinburgh University Press, Edinburgh, 1970).

[16] Since one knows in advance that this is precisely what selecting a sentiency criterion will do, one must be prepared to sanction such discrimination. That is, one knows that a sentiency criterion will advantage ourselves and the 'higher' animals and disadvantage everything else, which is exactly what Singer's speciesist does, only in respect of advantaging ourselves alone. As I say, a sentiency criterion for the possession of rights merely broadens the class of those licensed to discriminate.

to endow nature with experiences or mental states,[17] they are likely to regard a sentiency criterion for the possession of rights, which is a major hope of animal rightists, as retarding their cause. After all, the countless species of plants and trees, for example, profit not in the least from a concern with mental states.

More is at issue here, however, than merely being able to turn the charge of discrimination in upon animal rightists and liberationists. For, lacking experiences or mental states, the things which make up non-sentient creation lack not only moral rights but also what I shall call moral standing. By this, I mean that, in the absence of experiences or mental states, they are not themselves the bearers or repositories of value in their own right; they have, in a word, no value in themselves. Feinberg, who is an animal rightist, is emphatic about this:

A mere thing, however valuable to others, has no good of its own. The explanation of that fact, I suspect, consists in the fact that mere things have no conative life. . . . Interests must be compounded somehow out of conations; hence mere things have no interests. *A fortiori*, they have no interests to be protected by legal or moral rules. Without interests a creature can have no "good" of its own, the achievement of which can be its due. Mere things are not loci of value in their own right, but rather their value consists entirely in their being objects of other beings' interests.[18]

Feinberg's position here is this: mere things are not loci of

---

[17] Some recent studies have suggested that plants can have experiences or mental states in this sense, that they can have awareness of their environment through primary perception. In addition to the popular book *The Secret Life of Plants* (Harper & Row, New York, 1973) by P. Tomkins and C. Bird, there is also Cleve Backster's well-known study 'Evidence of a Primary Perception in Plant Life' (*International Journal of Parapsychology*, x (1968), 329–48). See also K.A. Horowitz *et al.*, 'Plant "Primary Perception": Electrophysiological Unresponsiveness to Brine Shrimp Killing', *Science*, 189 (1975), 478–80; and J. Kmetz, 'A Study of Primary Perception in Plant and Animal Life', *Journal of the American Society of Psychical Research*, 71 (1977), 157–9. These works are generally critical of Backster and cast doubt upon the success of his experiments. I am grateful to H.M. Collins, of the University of Bath, for providing me with a copy of his unpublished paper 'Upon the Replication of Scientific Findings', which also is critical of Backster. I think it is fair to say that, though Backster has not been finally refuted, the case for primary perception in plants is yet to be made. (I am grateful to Michael Martin for bringing this material to my attention and discussing it with me.)

[18] J. Feinberg, 'The Rights of Animals and Unborn Generations', p. 50.

value in their own right because they lack interests, and they lack interests because they lack a conative life, which, as we saw earlier, he includes under 'sentience'; ultimately, therefore, it is because they lack sentiency that they have no good of their own and are not loci of value in their own right.[19] In this way, because the things which comprise it lack a good of their own and are not loci of value in their own right, non-sentient creation comes to lack even moral standing. Plainly, sentient creation is favoured, and whatever value non-sentient creation has lies in its relation to the interests of sentient creation; as Rodman puts it, 'nature is left in a state of thinghood, having no intrinsic value, acquiring instrumental value only as resources . . . for a sentient elite',[20] a conclusion which mirrors Hampshire's remark that a mental state view of value renders nature 'just machinery, useful or harmful in proportion as it promotes or prevents desired states of feeling'.[21]

If the beings which comprise sentient creation are loci of value in their own right, it is on the sentiency criterion because of their having experiences or mental states. Accordingly, what appears to be at the very basis of a sentiency criterion is the view that having experiences or mental states is valuable in its own right. It is just because the beings which comprise sentient creation do and/or can have experiences or mental states that they have moral standing and so are in a position to possess moral rights.

What, then, is the support animal rightists bring for the view that having experiences or mental states is valuable in its own right? I have been unable to find any in their writings; and the truth of the matter, in fact, is that they *implicitly assume* that having experiences or mental states is valuable in its own right. Indeed, I think they have to assume this; for unless one either argues for or assumes that having experiences or mental states is valuable in its own right and suffices to confer moral standing upon creatures who have or are capable of having them, what reason has one for thinking that sentiency is a criterion for the possession of *moral*

---

[19] Aspects of this position I return to and reject in Ch. VII.
[20] See Rodman, 'The Liberation of Nature?', 91; also below, p. 165.
[21] *Morality and Pessimism*, p. 3.

rights at all, that sentiency has anything whatever to do with morality?

Put differently, why are shrubs (i) not loci of value in their own right and (ii) completely lacking in moral rights? It would make no sense for Feinberg to say that it is because they lack this or that *kind* of experiences or mental states, such as hopes or experiences of pain; for the whole point is that plants, trees, shrubs, forests, valleys, etc. lack any and all kinds of experiences and mental states whatever. They are not non-sentient because they lack this or that kind of mental state but because they lack mental states altogether; and it is this fact which, on a sentiency criterion, denies them moral standing and places them beyond the realm of those things, as Feinberg would have it, which have a good the achievement of which can be their due. (Thus, having a good, on Feinberg's view, is dependent upon having experiences, a thesis which I dispute in Chapter VII.)

In this way, then, the implicit assumption that having experiences or mental states is valuable in its own right lies at the very basis of a sentiency criterion and is used to confer moral standing and moral rights upon one part of creation and to refuse them to another. Quite simply, an assumption of this magnitude and importance to the cause of animal rights requires argument in its support: it is by no means obviously true, nor can I see any immediate reason to give way in the fact of it. For if asked to name those things one regarded as intrinsically valuable, I think many people would reply that, *if anything* is intrinsically valuable, in order by this formulation to leave open the very real possibility, which philosophers and others have argued for, that nothing is, then such things as deep and lasting friendships in the fullest of senses and the development of one's talents are. What I strongly suspect is that virtually no one would cite having experiences or mental states *per se* as among the class of the intrinsically valuable.

I shall end on a different but closely related note, which I shall take up again in Chapter XI. Sentient beings have an enormous number of different kinds of experiences, and by no means all or even a substantial minority of them are experiences of pain; so why, as so many animal rightists do,

48   MENTAL STATES AND MORAL STANDING

single out experiences of pain from all the other kinds which
sentient beings have? Because, it will be said, experiences of
pain are themselves possessed of intrinsic value, i.e. are intrinsically evil. For the moment, this answer warrants three
observations, the last two of which bring out and emphasize
what I feel to be a certain arbitrariness in isolating experiences
of pain in this way.

(1) Argument is needed to establish that experiences of
pain *are* possessed of intrinsic value; merely to assume that
they are will not do, and appeals to authority, such as that
Bentham and others have held that they are, beg the question.

For example, in saying that pain is an intrinsic evil, some
people have meant that it is undesirable in itself. Without
going into complex detail, my point is this: either the sentence 'Pain is undesirable in itself' is analytic and so results,
if denied, in a contradiction or it is synthetic and experience
(and argument) is required in order to substantiate its truth.
I find nothing contradictory in someone liking a pain to
which he has nevertheless given his full attention; indeed, I
think Hare, in his paper 'Pain and Evil', has shown this not to
be contradictory and has successfully disputed the alleged
analyticity of 'Pain is undesirable in itself'.[22] The truth of
this claim remains to be shown.

Importantly, moreover, claims that this or that is of intrinsic value must also be able to meet the arguments of John
Dewey,[23] Monroe Beardsley,[24] and a host of others that
there is nothing possessed of intrinsic value and/or that the
notion lacks a clear analysis, if it is not actually incoherent.
The concept of intrinsic value, in fact, is a difficult and controversial one, a point which, as J.J.C. Smart has recently recalled to our attention in his paper 'Hedonistic and Ideal
Utilitarianism',[25] continues to plague act-utilitarians in the
statement and defence of their theories, many of which

[22] In *Essays on the Moral Concepts* (Macmillan, London, 1972), pp. 76–91.
[23] *Theory of Valuation* (University of Chicago Press, Chicago, 1939), pp. 26–9.
[24] 'Intrinsic Value', *Philosophy and Phenomenological Research*, 26 (1965), 1–17.
[25] J.J.C. Smart, 'Hedonistic and Ideal Utilitarianism', *Midwest Studies in Philosophy*, iii (1978), 240–51.

incorporate and rely upon the view that pain is an intrinsic evil. Nor am I aware that those philosophers who regard value completely instrumentally, according to which something is valuable to the degree to which it satisfies or is conducive to satisfying (human) wants, interests, and purposes, which can vary from person to person, are simply *obviously* wrong.

(2) Even if experiences of pain are possessed of intrinsic value, it does not follow that other kinds of experiences are not also possessed of intrinsic value; and if they are, why should not the sentiency criterion be formulated in terms of (one of) them?

For example, G.E. Moore's *Principia Ethica* became well-known, especially through the Bloomsbury Group, to a non-philosophical public, partly through Moore's insistence that experiences based upon the contemplation of beauty were intrinsically valuable.[26] It would require a good deal of argument, however, to show that even the 'higher' animals engage in the contemplation of beauty. In other words, though only sentient creatures can have experiences of beauty, since such experiences presuppose the power of sense-perception, *not all* sentient creatures can have such experiences. Why, then, if one is determined to adopt a sentiency criterion, should it be formulated around experiences of pain and so be animal-including instead of being formulated around experiences of beauty and so be animal-excluding? The point is not peculiar to experiences of beauty; for the present question can be raised in respect of *any* kind of experiences which is such that (i) it is held to be possessed of intrinsic value, (ii) it is had only by sentient creatures but not by all such creatures, i.e. not by the 'higher' animals, and (iii) it is other than and does not amount to feeling pain.

(It is perhaps worth mentioning that the exercise of free will and of moral agency has a long history in this connection with a sentiency criterion. For if only sentient creatures can exercise free will and moral agency, and this is not an implausible assumption, it nevertheless remains the case that not all sentient creatures can. In this way, sentiency might be held to be in some sense a ground for rights, but animals

---

[26] *Principia Ethica* (Cambridge University Press, Cambridge, 1959), Ch. VI.

would still be excluded from the class of right-holders. Readers will find that attacks on this position nearly always rely upon the dubious argument from marginal cases in order to refute or undermine it.)

(3) If more kinds of experiences than merely experiences of pain are (held to be) possessed of intrinsic value, yet if animal rightists nevertheless want to give moral pride of place to experiences of pain in the formulation of the sentiency criterion, on what justified basis do they do this? I am aware of no answer to this question in the writings of animal rightists, though this is perhaps not surprising, in view of the fact that the sorts of questions raised here are not usually raised by them. But some answer or other must be forthcoming, and a word of warning on what I suspect will be the most common answer is necessary.

This answer consists in citing the role experiences of pain play in producing the responses to their environment so characteristic of higher sentient life. Such an answer amounts to giving moral pride of place to experiences of pain for a naturalistic-cum-evolutionary reason which, so far as I can see, has no apparent moral status whatever, any more than a naturalistic-cum-evolutionary account of why and how chameleons adapt to their environment partly through changes in colour has moral status. It may perhaps be that on some evolutionary normative ethic this evolutionary role of experiences of pain *can be endowed* with moral significance; but, though I myself am inclined to agree with Antony Flew that such theories are open to serious, if not conclusive, objections,[27] it is in any event clear that this alleged endowment is inextricably linked to the question of the acceptability of evolutionary normative ethics. Reject the theories, and experiences of pain no longer have the moral significance they are here alleged to have.

I have in the last two observations been arguing that a certain arbitrariness is involved in seizing upon experiences of pain as the terms in which to formulate a sentiency criterion;

---

[27] *Evolutionary Ethics* (Macmillan, London, 1967), especially Chs. III and IV. Doubtless the most prominent reason evolutionary theories have been dismissed in recent years is the conviction that they commit the naturalistic fallacy. For an argument in support of the view that they do, see *Evolutionary Ethics*, pp. 37–51.

the same point, however, can be made in a different and much more direct way. In the hands of animal rightists, a sentiency criterion, as I see it, seeks for the lowest common denominator between men and the 'higher' animals,[28] endows or follows others in endowing this denominator, i.e. pain, with moral significance, and uses it to confer moral standing and moral rights upon one part of creation while denying them to another. (This, I suspect, is why experiences of beauty will quickly be discarded: they are, so to speak, not 'low' enough to serve the animal rightist's purpose here.) But *why* should we seek for the lowest common denominator? It is not laid down in heaven that we must. Nor are we inconsistent if we do not; there is nothing to be inconsistent with. The real answer, of course, is that, if we do not seek for the lowest common denominator, animals are unlikely to be included within the class of right-holders; but this is no answer at all, to one who is unsure whether animals possess moral rights and who requires an argument to quiet his doubts.

Nor must we forget Rodman and other environmentalists, whose complaints here will be slightly different. If we do undertake a search for a lowest common denominator, upon the basis of which to formulate a criterion for the possession of moral rights, why, they will urge, must the search be restricted to ourselves and a few other species, i.e. the 'higher' animals, instead of being widened to include the innumerable species of plants, trees, etc.? Since the search is undertaken in the first place in order to combat discrimination, by trying to force the inclusion of animals within the class of right-holders, why should the search be artificially restricted to only a very few, favoured species, when the result is bound to be merely another form of discrimination? Why, especially, as Michael A. Fox has suggested to me, if the search is worth undertaking in the first place, should it not at the very least be carried out over the class of what we regard as living things, which includes not only human beings and the 'higher'

---

[28] This is how the point is usually put in discussion; it is reflected as well, as we shall see in Ch. VI, in Russell's behaviouristic account of the root essence of desire as something shared between human beings and animals. See also Rodman, op. cit. 123.

animals but also, for example, the 'lower' animals, plants, trees, and, what Fox urges most especially, ecological systems generally? Fox's suggestion is increasingly pressed by environmentalists against the use of a sentiency criterion by animal rightists, for obvious reasons; and I suspect a good many people who are by no means rabid environmentalists are increasingly coming to feel its impact. After all, is there not something disquieting about a criterion for the possession of moral rights which, as Hampshire would put it, turns everything else in creation except that which can have mental states 'into machinery', to be used by whatever can have mental states just as any other piece of machinery is used by them?

(Though I have used Rodman, Fox and others who have a concern with the environment in the last part of this chapter in order to bring out (i) the discriminatory use of experiences or mental states as the basis for possessing moral standing, (ii) the lack of argument to show that having experiences or mental states *per se* really is valuable in its own right, and (iii) the arbitrary selection of experiences of pain as the terms in which to formulate a sentiency criterion for the possession of rights, I do not wish at all to imply that they would support my attack on animal rights. Almost certainly, they would not.)

V

Interests and their Analysis

Nelson's argument, to recall, is this:

All and only beings which (can) have interests (can) have moral rights;
Animals as well as humans (can) have interests;
Therefore, animals (can) have moral rights.

As I remarked in Chapter I, if this argument is successfully to include animals within the class of right-holders, then the truth of its minor premiss is essential; but Nelson's own views on the matter, even though his name is fondly recalled by many animal rightists, are not very helpful, and for three reasons.

(1) In *A System of Ethics*, Nelson argues that the contention that we cannot *know* whether animals have interests is irrelevant, since he has, he says, 'defined animals as carriers of interests'.[1] Given this definition, and given that beings which have interests have moral rights, it follows that animals have such rights; but the use of what amounts to a stipulative definition in order to obtain the truth of this result spoils the result itself. For Nelson does not show but in effect simply asserts that animals have interests, and no one dubious in the first place on this score is likely to be persuaded otherwise by mere assertion.

(2) Reliance upon definition in this way obviates the necessity for Nelson to cite the necessary and sufficient conditions for a being to have interests, with the result that we

---

[1] L. Nelson, *A System of Ethics*, p. 139; see also J. Passmore, *Man's Responsibility for Nature*, p. 116.

have no way of checking to see if his assertion that animals
do have interests is in fact true. Nor can a list of such conditions be extracted from the text. For example, the notion
of rationality will not do, since Nelson specifically defines
animals as 'carriers of interests' and as 'non-rational';[2] the
notion of being a living creature will not do, since he appears
quite prepared to accept that stones *may* have interests;[3] the
notion of consciousness will not do, since he appears prepared to accept that cabbages *may* have interests;[4] and the
notion of responding to stimuli will not do, since he allows
that electric bells respond to stimuli but do not have interests.[5] The notion of pain will not do, since Nelson is prepared to allow that stones, cabbages, trees, and shrubs *may*
have interests; very few people, however, have ever thought
these things to be capable of being in pain, which, in any
event, they could not be, unless they were possessed of
consciousness. Nor will being a person do, since Nelson identifies the notion of being a person with that of being a carrier
of interests;[6] in other words, they are the same notion, a
view which commits Nelson to regarding animals and,
possibly, stones and cabbages as persons, something also
which has not usually been thought. In short, because he
does not specify the conditions in virtue of which animals as
well as humans have interests, we cannot check to see if
animals do indeed meet those conditions; in the end, we are
left in the unsatisfactory position of having only Nelson's
assertion that they do, without having been given any reason
to think this assertion true.

(3) Most importantly of all, Nelson nowhere analyses the
concept of an interest, so that we are not told *what it is* that
men and animals are alleged to have when they are alleged to
have interests. The absence of such an analysis is puzzling in
the extreme: Nelson's whole position on the moral rights of
animals turns upon his claim that they have interests, and
there is simply no way of coming to grips with this claim
unless we know what an interest is.

These, then, are three significant difficulties with Nelson's

---

[2] *A System of Ethics*, p. 138.   [3] Ibid. 140.   [4] Ibid. 140.
[5] Ibid. 141.   [6] Ibid. 138.

own treatment of the minor premiss of his argument, and I take it as obvious that the third of these — failure to analyse the concept of an interest — is absolutely critical to the whole (philosophical) enterprise of showing that animals have interests.

Traditionally, the most favoured approach to the analysis of the concept of an interest has linked interests to desires. Such, for example, is Feinberg's view, as we saw in the last chapter: he holds that things are not loci of value in their own right because they lack interests, and they lack interests because they lack a conative life, by which he understands such things as having wishes and desires. I can best begin to develop, in order eventually to make use of, certain elements in this traditional approach through a discussion of Tom Regan's criticisms of Feinberg's position. My remarks should be understood as prefatory to what follows in subsequent chapters; for though I shall defend Feinberg against Regan's criticisms, I do not agree with Feinberg's position on several important essentials, as will later become apparent.

In his seminal paper 'The Rights of Animals and Unborn Generations',[7] Feinberg indicates his acceptance of the interest requirement (Nelson's major premiss) and then proceeds to try to puzzle out who can and cannot have interests. He takes interests to be compounded out of desires (and aims), desires to presuppose beliefs (a point which I shall make use of in Chapters VI and VII), and, for example, plants and cars to be incapable of having beliefs, since they lack even rudimentary cognitive equipment. He also specifies the sorts of beliefs he thinks are presupposed by desires: he instances being able to form beliefs of the types 'If I want X, then I must do Y' and 'Since I want X, and Y appears to be X, then I must get Y'. In his reply, 'Feinberg On What Sorts of Beings Can Have Rights',[8] Regan examines two principles for the ascription of rights — the interest and the goodness principles — which he finds in Feinberg's essay. What Regan wants to establish is that it would be premature for anyone to accept either principle, at least in the state Feinberg has

---

[7] In *Philosophy and Environmental Crisis*, ed. W.T. Blackstone, pp. 43–68.
[8] *Southern Journal of Philosophy* (Winter 1976), 485–98.

left them, and that the two principles lead to inconsistent results, so far as which beings can and which cannot possess rights. Nearly all of Regan's paper is devoted to the goodness principle; with respect to the interest principle, which is nothing more than Nelson's major premiss, understood in the light of Feinberg's analysis of interests, Regan deploys two arguments in support of his contention that it would be premature to accept Feinberg's traditional posture on interests, neither of which I find conclusive.

(1) Regan contends that there are some beings who can have desires but cannot form beliefs of the types in question. He claims, for instance, that severely disoriented, retarded, but sentient children can desire something to ease the pain of an abscessed tooth, even though they cannot form beliefs of the requisite kinds.[9]

Regan contends that it would be 'grotesque'[10] to say that these children do not have this desire and, later, that it is 'plain'[11] that they can desire things. I myself find neither the one thing grotesque nor the other plain; but since it might be maintained that pursuing this tack could at best only show that my intuitions do not agree with Regan's in the matter, I shall develop a different line of reply.

I do not object in principle to the use of our intuitions in order to evaluate claims of Regan's sort; but the worth of this means of evaluation is sharply reduced the more the case or cases under consideration depart from ordinary, normal ones. If, for example, Feinberg's analysis of interests yielded the result that normal adult humans could not have desires because they could not form beliefs of the relevant types, then our very clear intuitions on the matter would doubtless lead us to reflect again upon the adequacy of Feinberg's analysis. But Regan's is by no means an ordinary, normal case, and our intuitions about it are for that very reason both more likely to vary from person to person and to be far less clear than in the usual cases.

As a result, a hard-line response to Regan's claim can be envisaged: if interests are analysed in terms of desires and desires at least partially in terms of beliefs of specified sorts,

[9] Ibid. 487.   [10] Ibid. 487.   [11] Ibid. 488.

then beings who cannot form beliefs of the requisite sorts just do not have desires. I can perhaps best bring out the nature and force of this sort of reply by means of an example from the tennis world, where a former male player, as the result of a sex change, at present seeks to compete in the female division. If a particular tournament authority analyses or lays down what it is to be a woman in terms of a certain genetic test, and if a player cannot pass that test, then *whatever else may be said in support* of that player's female candidacy, that player is not a woman to that tournament authority. Perhaps on some other, some lesser test (for example, physical appearance) that player will be a woman; but on the test specified, if a player fails it, then that player is not a woman. And that is the end of the matter, so far as this particular tournament authority is concerned.

If the hard-liner sticks to his guns, then, he is going to doubt that the children Regan describes have desires. It is bound to be suggested, however, that all that is necessary to ensure that they do have desires is to give up either the link between desire and beliefs of the requisite sorts or the link between desire and belief itself. In other words, as in the tennis example, adopting some other, perhaps some lesser standard can be made to yield the wanted result.

But why, on the strength of the sort of case Regan has provided, *should* we give up the one link or the other? Let us revert to the tennis example again. The genetic test the tournament authority imposed gave the result that the player who had undergone the sex change failed and that Chris Evert and Virginia Wade passed. Now what would make the tournament authority give up this test? Whatever else would, it seems certain that the genetic test would be given up if Chris Evert, Virginia Wade, and a succession of other players in the female division failed it as well. In other words, if not only the deviant cases but also the normal ones were excluded from the female division by a test to determine who was and who was not a woman, then that test would be given up. But if we look at the case of desire and belief, we find that Feinberg's analysis includes normal adult humans within the class of those who have desires while placing in doubt the inclusion of those deviant humans among us whom Regan has seized upon; and this result, I should have thought, is not particularly shocking. In short, since the analysis covers the normal cases, why should the sort of case Regan presents induce even the soft-liners among us to give up the link between desire and beliefs of the requisite sorts or the link between desire and belief itself? Certainly, appeal to deviant cases is not going to rattle the hard-liner.

There is a further point here that warrants attention. Are these severely disoriented, retarded, but sentient children, who are said to be able to desire something to ease the pain of an abscessed tooth, able to form beliefs of some sort or other but not of Feinberg's requisite sorts? Or are they able to form no beliefs whatever? It is not always clear to me which of these things Regan has in mind; either one, however, demands support. If these children are held to be able to form beliefs of some sort or other but not of Feinberg's sorts, then the analysis of desire in terms of belief is not necessarily overthrown; for example, it might turn out, as the result of further argument on Regan's part, that Feinberg has simply misidentified the sorts of beliefs required in order to have desires. Equally importantly, however, and I think this should be stressed, something is then going to have to be said about the sorts of beliefs these children allegedly *do* have; for one of Feinberg's requisite sorts – 'If I want X, then I must do Y' – certainly *appears basic to any analysis* of desire. If, however, these severely disoriented and retarted children are held to be able to form no beliefs whatever, then I think we simply must have some statement of Regan's own analysis of desire, if we are to be in a position to assess, let alone agree with, his claim that these children nevertheless do have desires.

(2) Regan contends that, on the analysis of desire in terms of beliefs, the beliefs must be connected to the desires in such a way that, for example, one's capacity to form the belief 'Grannie knits afghans' is not a sufficient basis for supposing one desires to swim the English Channel; and he implies that this — how beliefs become allied to the relevant desires — is a problem which has yet to be solved.

This, I think, is largely a pseudo-problem. Suppose I am a book-collector and collect first editions of E.M. Forster: I own a first edition of every novel he published except

Howards End. I believe my collection lacks a first edition of this work, and, given my aim of owning first editions of all Forster's novels, I desire one. Now if someone were to ask why my belief that my collection lacks a first edition of *Howards End* is connected with my desire to own a first edition of *Howards End* and not with a desire to swim the English Channel, what better or more direct reply can be given than that, without the belief that my collection does not contain a first edition of *Howards End,* I would not desire one, whereas without this belief I may or may not desire (and continue to desire) to swim the English Channel? Once I obtain a first edition of *Howards End,* my desire to own one is satisfied, whereas any desire I might have to swim the English Channel is certainly not satisfied by my acquisition of the novel, unless, of course, and this is the only proviso we need bother with here, some unusual circumstance has led me so intimately to associate in my mind owning a first edition of *Howards End* and swimming the English Channel that, if this is possible, provided I accomplish one or the other deed, both desires are satisfied. (Quite how this would work, so that swimming the English Channel completely satisfied my desire to own a first edition of *Howards End,* I do not know.) My point here is the not unfamiliar one that the objects of desires play an integral role in our individuating one desire from another, and one test of the object of a desire is what meets, fulfils and ultimately removes our having the desire.

For these reasons, then, I do not find Regan's two arguments against Feinberg's traditional analysis conclusive. As with the argument from marginal cases, so here also we find a case — and a deviant case at that — being taken for granted, in order to provide a basis upon which to erect doubts and objections.

Regan does not consider the hard-line response to his claim sketched above; and the explanation for this may be that he thinks it follows, if only he can extract from us the concession that severely disoriented and retarded children have wants, that these children who cannot form beliefs or beliefs of the requisite sorts therefore have desires. But even if his opponents are prepared to concede that these children have wants, it does not follow from the fact that they want X that they desire X. Not all wants are desires: to give only the most obvious example, the traditional analysis of interests is normally conducted in terms of desires and not in terms of needs, another class of wants but with marked dissimilarities to desires. (I shall explore this distinction in the next chapter.) Nor does it follow from the fact that these children want in the sense of 'need' something for the pain that they want in the sense of 'desire' something for the pain; for this to follow, Regan is going to have to stipulate some analysis of the concepts in question which gives such a result.

Are Regan's opponents, however, going to concede that these severely disoriented and retarded children can want something to relieve the pain in a sense of 'want' other than 'need'? At least in part, the answer is going to depend upon the general analysis they give of what it is to want something. A single example should suffice to make the point.

In *Action, Emotion and Will,* Anthony Kenny argues that a sentence of the form 'I want X' specifies a want for X, where X is a tangible object, such as a pill or shot for the relief of pain, only if the following conditions obtain: (a) something which is an X will satisfy the desire; (b) something which is not an X will not satisfy the desire better or as well; (c) the speaker or wanter can provide an answer to the question 'What counts as getting X?'; (d) the speaker or wanter can provide an answer to the question 'What do you want X for?'; and (e) X is not known already by the speaker or wanter to be in his power.[12] Can the children Regan describes meet these conditions? Probably not, in so far as these conditions involve (self-) knowledge, some experience of the world which one has digested, possible sophisticated verbalization or interior speech, and somewhat complicated means–end reasoning. It is fashionable to add today as well that wanting takes place under a description, that, for example, Oedipus wants the death of the arrogant stranger before him but not the death of his father. Under what descriptions, however, do severely disoriented and retarded

[12] A. Kenny, *Action, Emotion and Will* (Routledge & Kegan Paul, London, 1963), pp. 100–26.

children want a shot for the relief of pain? Are they able to cognize their experience sufficiently to make it feasible to impute even such relatively unsophisticated descriptions as the above to them? At best, the answers are unclear. Why, then, should a proponent of this analysis go on to concede that severely disoriented and retarded children have wants other than needs? In particular, since the analysis covers the ordinary, normal cases of wanting in adult humans, why should its proponent concede that appeal to a deviant case, one which is simply taken for granted as a case of wanting other than needing, undermines or even impairs the analysis? My point, of course, is not that we should endorse Kenny's analysis but that Regan's conviction — that these children do have wants — is not only not transparently true but may also be open to doubt, once an analysis of wanting is specified.

The traditional analysis of interests which I have found in Feinberg and defended against Regan I now want to explore and make use of in the case against Nelson's minor premiss. In any event, within this traditional analysis, the hard-liner I have sketched in this chapter does think that the unfortunate children Regan describes have needs; and the relationship of needs to interests, and the possibility of using such a relationship in order to show that animals have interests, require that we move to block this route to a defence of the Nelsonian minor premiss.

VI

Needs and the
Essence of Desire

Before going further, I want briefly to enlarge upon my discussion of needs in the preceding chapter. I shall do so in the course of considering a behaviouristic interpretation of the essence of desire, in which my aim is to show (i) how, by defending one such interpretation against its most powerful objection, the question of whether animals have desires quite naturally arises and (ii) how this question might receive a negative answer. It is *not* my concern, however, to adopt a behaviouristic interpretation of the essence of desire, and the reason I do not will become apparent in the next chapter.

Both Anthony Kenny in *Action, Emotion and Will*[1] and David Pears in his paper 'Russell's Theory of Desire'[2] are highly critical of Bertrand Russell's theory of desire, and especially of Russell's view of the essence of desire, which he regards as something shared between human beings and animals. At bottom, they object to Russell's behaviourism, though Pears does question whether *all* passages in Lecture III ('Desire and Feeling') of *The Analysis of Mind*[3] show that Russell subscribed undeviatingly to a behaviouristic line. But it is beyond doubt that the reduction of desire to behaviour is explicitly argued for in Lecture III,[4] and both Kenny and Pears direct the same, powerful objection to such a reduction.

---

[1] Ch. 3.
[2] In Pears's *Questions in the Philosophy of Mind* (Duckworth, London, 1975), pp. 251-71.
[3] B. Russell, *The Analysis of Mind* (George Allen & Unwin, London, 1921), pp. 58-76. Hereafter abbreviated to *AM*.
[4] Pears accepts this much: 'Russell's Theory of Desire', 255-6.

I want to suggest, however, that a Russellian view of the essence of desire can withstand the Kenny–Pears objection and in a way which is highly illuminating with regard to my aims in this book. The view set out is Russellian and not Russell's, first, because it contains significant additions to Russell's view, and second, because it unfolds with an emphasis and from a point of view which were not Russell's.

A word about this emphasis and point of view is necessary at the outset. Russell, Kenny, and Pears all concern themselves with animal desire in order to acquire points of comparison and contrast for the analysis and understanding of human desire, particularly conscious human desire; and both Kenny and Pears agree that Russell's view of the essence of desire is hardly defensible in respect of conscious human desire. My concern, however, is simply with the alleged desires of *animals*, with whether a Russellian line in *this* regard is defensible. I am going to argue that, with some additions, it *is* defensible, specifically, that it can meet the important objection which Kenny and Pears direct against it. Since these additions are an essential part of the rebuttal, however, the resultant view of animal desire is Russellian and not Russell's.

Everything in Russell's account of the essence of desire springs, I think, from his conviction that animals have desires but do not have minds (or, at least, cannot be known to have minds).[5] This is one of the central tenets of Russell's philosophy of mind, as expounded in *The Analysis of Mind*, and determines in its entirety his account of the essence of desire and, therefore, animal desire. For the immediate upshot of this central tenet is that the essence of desire cannot be such as either to make essential and necessary reference to a mind or to be in any way dependent upon the possession of a mind. An enormous number of possible analyses of the essence of desire are hereby excluded. The only one Russell discusses at any length in his lecture is that of desire as the

[5] *AM* 61–2. Lest I give rise to a misleading impression, i.e. that I have found passages in Lecture III overlooked by Kenny and Pears, I should perhaps state at the outset that not only is this not the case but that I notice many of the same passages they do. It is not such overlooked passages, but the case for the view, to which this chapter builds, that animals have needs but not desires, that I am after here.

prevision of the ends which desires achieve, which prevision
moves the agent to action:[6] since animals have desires but
not minds, and since it is only their behaviour and never their
previsions or thoughts with which we are directly acquainted,
it follows that desire does not consist in the prevision of the
ends desires achieve but that 'actions alone must be the test
of the desires of animals'.[7] However, other possible analyses
of the essence of desire are also excluded.

For example, the essence of desire cannot consist in or in
any way make essential reference to mental states (or acts or
activities), unless this phrase is treated in such a way as to
allow a being to have mental states without having a mind.
Russell puts the point succinctly:

> The characteristic mark by which we recognize a series of actions which
> display hunger is not the animal's mental state, which we cannot ob-
> serve, but something in its bodily behaviour; it is this observable trait
> in the bodily behaviour that I am proposing to call "hunger", not some
> possibly mythical and certainly unknowable ingredient of the animal's
> mind.[8]

Again, the essence of desire cannot consist in or in any way
make essential reference to choices and decisions, where
these are understood to rest upon or involve deliberation or
rational decision-procedures or reason-based action. Thus,
any view of wants in which to want to do something is to
have reasons which incline or move one to act must be rejected, unless the phrase 'having a reason' is treated in such a
way that beings without minds can have reasons. Or again,
the essence of desire cannot consist in or in any way make
essential reference to sensations. What Kenny calls the
'empiricist' account of the essence of desire, according to
which desire is thought of 'as a particular indefinable sensation, whose unanalysable nature can be grasped by each of us
only by a mental gaze upon our own experience',[9] must be
rejected. From an animal's observed behaviour we cannot
infer that it is led to behave as it does by a sensation, which
we can never penetrate to or identify; and merely to assume,
on analogy with the case of human beings, that sensations are

---

[6] *AM* 61–3.   [7] *AM* 62.   [8] *AM* 63.
[9] A. Kenny, *Action, Emotion and Will*, p. 101.

the starting-points of animal behaviour overlooks the many instances of *human* behaviour where sensations are not the starting-point, do not accompany the behaviour, and, indeed, have not even occurred.

In Lecture III, Russell does not deny that there may be sensations accompanying animal behaviour; but since we think that animals have desires, yet find we are unable to penetrate their behaviour *to* their sensations, desire cannot consist in or make essential reference to sensations. Strictly speaking, however, if Russell does allow that animals may have sensations, and that these sensations may accompany animal behaviour, then even if he is entitled to conclude that animal desire cannot *consist* in having such sensations, he is not equally entitled to conclude that animal desire (and the essence of desire) cannot make *essential reference* to them. For if they do occur, we have no seeming justification for excluding them *a priori* as part of the essence of desire. As Pears notes, however, in Lecture XV of *The Analysis of Mind*, Russell does go on to argue that sensations 'are the sort of thing of which we *may* be conscious, but not a sort of thing of which we *must* be conscious';[10] but since we cannot penetrate to that consciousness which may allegedly underlie animal behaviour, and since we are directly acquainted only with the behaviour itself, it would seem to follow that we cannot know that animals have sensations, in which case, since we do think they have desires, it is not to their having or to the possibility of their having sensations to which we refer when we ascribe desires to them. This is a stronger argument than the previous one, and an attempted justification of the claim that the essence of desire does not consist in and does not make essential reference to either felt sensations or their possibility.

The question of whether the behaviour of animals can be taken as evidence for the existence of sensations in them is not directly considered by Russell; but, as we saw in the case of hunger, he not only does not argue evidentially from behaviour to sensations but also holds this kind of 'détour

---

[10] *AM* 288; italics in original. See this entire section, pp. 287–90, for a fuller discussion of the matter.

through the animal's supposed mind' to be 'wholly unnecessary'.[11] Hunger refers to an observable trait of an
animal's behaviour, not to some 'mythical and certainly un-
knowable ingredient of an animal's mind'; and it is just because sensations are the sort of thing of which a being can
and may be conscious that to argue evidentially from animal
behaviour to sensations is to begin to make such an unnecessary 'détour' through an animal's supposed mind.

Now it is by means of sensations or mental occurrences,
of which human beings are or can be conscious or aware, and
of the notion of discomfort, which is a causal property of
mental occurrences, consisting in the fact 'that the occurrence in question stimulates voluntary or reflex movements
tending to produce some more or less definite change involving the cessation of the occurrence',[12] that Russell distinguishes human from animal desire.[13] Thus, Russell never
endorses a strict behaviourism in respect of human desire,
but quite explicitly allows there to be mental occurrences or
'accompaniments' to human behaviour.[14] But these 'accompaniments' do not characterize the essence of desire, since
we cannot know that there are any such 'accompaniments'
in the case of animals; such 'accompaniments' serve, therefore, only to mark off conscious human desire from other
types (animal desires, unconscious human desires). So far as
the essence of desire and animal desire is concerned, then,
Russell's account appears wholly behaviouristic. Animal desire is not only revealed in but also consists in behaviour, in
behaviour-cycles, which Russell defines as 'a series of voluntary or reflex movements of an animal, tending to cause a
certain result, and continuing until that result is caused,
unless they are interrupted by death, accident, or some new
behaviour-cycle'.[15] The search for something underlying their
behaviour which is desire in animals leads us, on the other
hand, to attribute all sorts of mental phenomena to them,
phenomena which we can never verify that they have. Why,
then, take the step of attributing such phenomena — and, by
implication, minds — to them?

[11] AM 62.   [12] AM 71.   [13] AM 67-76.
[14] AM 68-70. See Kenny, op. cit. 103; Pears, op. cit. 254.
[15] AM 65.

To this analysis of the essence of desire in terms of behaviour and behaviour-cycles, Kenny and Pears have objected that, unless we possess an independent criterion of identity for a behaviour-cycle, we shall not be able to tell where one behaviour-cycle ends and another begins.[16] In essence, they provide us with two ways of bringing out the force of this objection.

First, the criterion of identity of a behaviour-cycle cannot be forward-looking, to the end of the cycle, since, as Kenny remarks, any particular cycle can be interrupted and abruptly concluded. For example, a monkey in search of food can be distracted by another monkey into sexual activity; the end of the cycle concerned with the search for food is not such activity but eating, yet the cycle actually concludes in this case in copulation. The criterion of identity of a behaviour-cycle, therefore, must surely be backward-looking, if we are ever going to distinguish between its end (food) and its actual point of conclusion (sex) in the case of the monkey.[17] Quite naturally, a backward-looking criterion will, as Pears maintains, look to that which sets off the behaviour-cycle in the first place. In the case of the monkey, then, it might be said that what sets off its food-seeking behaviour is the desire for food. But this desire cannot consist in yet another cycle of behaviour, else we have to go on to ask after what set *it* off, and a regress is set in motion; and this regress is a vicious one, since, so long as it remains in motion, we never come to what sets off the whole chain of behaviour and so to that which will provide our criterion of identity for a behaviour-cycle. If, however, the desire which initiates the monkey's behaviour does *not* consist in another cycle of behaviour, then Russell's strict behaviourism in respect of animal desire is vitiated.

Second, a behaviour-cycle must have an onset, something which sets it off. In the case of human beings, discomfort, a causal property of our sensations and mental occurrences, is alleged by Russell to perform this task; what, then, sets off

[16] Kenny, op. cit. 104–11; Pears, op. cit. 252–7.
[17] This way of putting the objection, together with the way it is rounded off here, owes a debt to Richard Wollheim; see his 'Needs, Desires and Moral Turpitude', in *Nature and Conduct,* ed. R.S. Peters (Macmillan, London, 1975), p. 166.

behaviour-cycles in animals? The point is not merely that Russell does not say; it is also that, if I read Pears correctly, by identifying animal desire with behaviour and excluding any mental 'phenomena' from the essence of desire, Russell appears to preclude the possibility of our supplying an onset. For whatever we cite will itself either be more behaviour, in which case we must go on to seek for what set *it* off, or some mental 'phenomenon' which Russell has already excluded from the essence of desire, since it is not a cycle of behaviour. In either case, we are left in the dark as to what sets off behaviour-cycles in animals; and since it is by means of what sets them off that we individuate and identify them, it follows that we cannot individuate and identify separate behaviour-cycles in animals, in terms of which, however, Russell has defined animal desire.

This is a powerful argument, and doubtless to many it will now seem that one good reason for attributing minds and mental phenomena to animals is to explain what Russell cannot, namely, to explain what it is that sets off behaviour-cycles in animals and so why it is that an animal behaves as it does. This move, however, is unnecessary; for a purely causal account of what sets off behaviour-cycles in animals can be given, an account which does not require that we attribute minds or mental phenomena to animals and which is, therefore, consonant with Russell's general view of the matter.

According to Pears, Russell unwisely passed from excluding a particular kind of initiating mental event from the essence of desire — the prevision of the ends which desires achieve — to excluding 'all kinds of initiating mental events'.[18] If I am right, Russell does indeed exclude from the essence of desire anything which either makes essential and necessary reference to a mind or is in any way dependent upon the possession of a mind, from which it follows that not one but all kinds of mental events are excluded as the initiating events of behaviour-cycles in animals. However, Pears later goes on, by way of summary, to say that Russell excluded all 'internal initiating events from the essence of desire'.[19] Now this is not the case: though Russell excludes

[18] Pears, op. cit. 256.
[19] Ibid. 257.

all kinds of mental events as initiating events of behaviour-
cycles in animals, mental events are not the only sorts of
things 'internal' to an animal, nor does Russell suppose that
they are. For example, in Lecture III, Russell says of animals
that we 'are prepared to admit that their instincts prompt
useful actions without any prevision of the ends which they
achieve';[20] that is, in their cases, 'the stimulus to the performance of each act is an impulsion from behind, not an
attraction from the future'.[21] Of a bird that reproduces and
rears its young, Russell writes:

> The bird does what it does, at each stage, because it has an impulse to
> that particular action, not because it perceives that the whole cycle of
> actions will contribute to the preservation of the species. The same
> considerations apply to other instincts. A hungry animal feels restless,
> and is led by instinctive impulses to perform the movements which
> give it nourishment; but the act of seeking food is not sufficient evi-
> dence from which to conclude that the animal has the thought of food
> in its "mind".[22]

Moreover, Russell accounts for the case of our monkey who
is interrupted in his search for food and turns to sexual
activity in terms of conflicts of impulses, the stronger of
which predominates.[23] Now Russell plainly did not think
that an animal's drives, instincts, and impulses were somehow 'external' to it; rather, he thought they were 'internal'
to it, and importantly, as in the passages quoted, explained
why the animal behaves as it does. But he neither writes nor
implies that an animal's drives, instincts, and impulses make
essential and necessary reference to a mind or in any way
depend upon the possession of a mind. In other words, the
animal acts without our first having to attribute a mind or
mental phenomena to it in order to explain *why* it acts as it
does; such a 'détour', from, say, instincts through minds to
behaviour, is 'wholly unnecessary'.

In view of this linkage of animal desire and the essence of
desire to drives, instincts, etc., it is no accident that, even in
the case of human beings, Russell appears attracted by
Freudian theory. For the view that at the very basis of the
human psyche are a concatenation of instinctive drives which

[20] *AM* 61. The statement made in n. 5 above applies here as well.
[21] *AM* 66.   [22] *AM* 66-7.   [23] *AM* 62.

demand release in as immediate a manner as possible either
bypasses or de-emphasizes the role of consciousness and
conscious desires in accounting for why people behave as
they do. Thus, at one point, Russell writes:

> While we are talking or reading, we may eat in complete unconscious-
> ness; but we perform the actions of eating just as we should if we were
> conscious, and they cease when our hunger is appeased. What we call
> "consciousness" seems to be a mere spectator of the process; even when
> it issues orders, they are usually, like those of a wise parent, just such as
> would have been obeyed even if they had not been given. This view
> may seem at first exaggerated, but the more our so-called volitions
> and their causes are examined, the more it is forced upon us.[24]

Russell's attraction to this particular strand of Freudian
theory does not prevent him from acknowledging, via the
notion of discomfort, that there *are* conscious as well as
unconscious human desires; but such desires are, as it were, a
peculiarly human superstructure erected upon a view of the
essence of desire and animal desire that posits no intervening
medium between drives, instincts, etc., and behaviour. Such
behaviour, according to Russell, is carried on by means of
these drives and instincts, and ends in their quiescence, except when they are interrupted and dominated by stronger
drives, instincts, etc.

Drives, instincts, etc. are normally considered appropriate
to needs and their satisfaction, so that I think we may fairly
characterize the Russellian position as locating the initiating
internal events of animal behaviour-cycles, which are carried
on by means of drives and the like, in the needs of animals.
What is it, then, to need something?

A tree, a car, a cat, and a man can all need water; but the
need does not make essential and necessary reference to a
mind, does not in any way depend upon the possession of a
mind, does not presuppose knowledge or awareness of the
need, and importantly, does not even presuppose consciousness. Rather, it makes essential and necessary reference, as
Kenny puts it,[25] to those conditions which define survival
and/or normal functioning in their respective cases: without
water, the tree, cat, and man will all die, and the car (and,

---

[24] *AM* 67.
[25] Kenny, op. cit. 45.

too, the cat and man) will not function normally. In order for these things to stand in need of water, it must be the case, obviously, that they lack water: a car with a full radiator does not need water, nor do cats and men who have just drunk their fill.[26] In order to lack water, however, it is not necessary that the car, cat, and man 'know' or 'be aware' or 'be conscious' of their lack; even things without minds and all forms of mental phenomena, even things which are non-conscious can lack something. Moreover, whether a tree, car, cat, or man lacks and needs water is independent of any 'beliefs' they may have to the contrary; they can stand in need of water whether or not they 'think' that they do. This is true even in the case of human beings: nearly all of the thousands of women who suffer from anorexia nervosa are in need of food, even though many of them believe that they are horribly fat and have, as a result, fallen into a diet which is killing them through enforced malnutrition and starvation.

If this is right, if needs make essential and necessary reference to conditions of survival and/or normal functioning, then the question of whether animals can have needs turns upon whether they can be deficient in that which is essential and necessary to their survival and/or normal functioning. And, of course, the Russellian accepts that they can be deficient in these respects, and that, therefore, they do have needs. But, as we have seen, accepting that they have needs does not require that the Russellian attribute minds, mental phenomena, beliefs, or, for that matter, consciousness to them. Rather, the need in the animal simply triggers off a cycle of behaviour by which to still the need; and Russell's mention of instincts, impulses, etc., which are 'internal' to the animal but not mental, can be seen as a suggestion as to how the cycle of behaviour, once set in motion, is sustained in existence and eventually concluded.

The reply to the Kenny–Pears objection, then, would appear to be this: it is by their needs that a Russellian individuates and identifies behaviour-cycles in animals. Such cycles begin with a need, are carried on and maintained in existence by drives, instincts, impulses, and the like, and are concluded

---

[26] This notion of a lack is explored in detail and with considerable insight by Wollheim, op. cit. 163 ff.

when these drives etc. become quiescent as the result of having met and fulfilled the need. Of course, a behaviour-cycle appropriate to one need may, as Kenny noted, interrupt that appropriate to another; but we still individuate each of the cycles by tracing it to the particular need in which it has its genesis. At no point in this process of individuation, however, is a 'détour' through the animal's supposed mind necessary.

Surely this result, however, that we individuate behaviour-cycles in animals by means of their needs, is what everyone — Kenny, Pears, and the rest of us — has thought all along was the case, at least upon study and reflection? So how can it be the reply to the Kenny–Pears objection? To see how, we must see how the Russellian responds to a further objection.

If animal desires are defined in terms of behaviour-cycles, and if behaviour-cycles are individuated by means of animal needs, then animal desires appear to collapse into animal needs. And this is surprising, since, in our own case, we have desires as well as needs. At the very least, therefore, the Russellian position on desire requires that we have an argument to show why the case of animals is so unlike our own. That is, why is it we can have wants as needs and wants as desires, whereas animals can have only wants as needs? I want briefly to sketch one possible answer to this objection.

As we have seen, in order to need something, I have to require it through being deficient in respect of it; in order to desire something, on the other hand, I have to judge or think or believe that I am deficient in respect of it, whether or not, and this must be stressed, I in fact am.[27] Suppose I am the collector of fine paintings and desire to own a Rembrandt: my desire to own a Rembrandt is to be traced to my belief that I do not now own one and that my art collection is deficient in this respect. If it turns out, contrary to what I believe, that my collection has had a Rembrandt in it all the time, then my desire to own a Rembrandt is to be traced to my false belief that, though I own many Old Masters, I own nothing by the hand of Rembrandt. Or consider again those

---

[27] See Wollheim, op. cit. 174. Presumably, this is a point which Feinberg also accepts, since, as we saw in the last chapter, he too holds the view that having desires requires having beliefs.

women who suffer from anorexia nervosa: many of these women desperately need food but do not desire it. They need food because they lack it, and this deficiency threatens both their normal functioning and survival; but they do not desire food because they believe that they are horribly fat and that eating will only exacerbate this condition. Though this belief is false, and they are in fact slowly starving to death, it nevertheless accounts for why they do not desire food. Finally, the man who desires to be a prominent philosopher believes, whether truly or falsely, that he is not yet prominent, or not yet sufficiently prominent, or not yet as prominent as three other philosophers he can name.

If this is right, if needs make essential and necessary reference to conditions of survival and/or normal functioning, whereas desires make essential and necessary reference to beliefs (a view of desires, as we saw earlier, which Feinberg also embraces), then the question of whether animals can have desires turns upon whether they can have beliefs; and here the Russellian has grave doubts. For unless the anti-Russellian is prepared to reduce belief to behaviour or in some other way to identify the two, he is likely to follow the traditional view that beliefs require a mental apparatus, that they either directly or indirectly make reference to a mind and mental phenomena, which at the very least, the Russellian urges, we do not know that animals have. Put summarily, then, animals cannot have beliefs unless they have minds, and they cannot have desires unless they have beliefs; but they can and do have needs whether or not they have beliefs, whether or not they have minds, whether or not they are aware of their deficiencies in particular respects, and whether or not they are even conscious.

Of course, the overwhelming temptation for the anti-Russellian is either to try to think up different kinds of desires and to hold that animals, even if they cannot have the above and countless other kinds, at least can have some kinds or to try to wring out of us the concession that animals *do have* beliefs, not, certainly, in some sense which requires the possession of complex and abstract concepts, but in some minimal or rudimentary sense. I shall defer until later a consideration of the former alternative and turn instead to the latter and, at least in this chapter, more pertinent one.

An example of a rudimentary belief in animals might be this: a squirrel, gathering nuts, walks out along the branch of a tree, and its behaviour indicates, it might be held, that it believes that the branch will not break or give way under its weight.[28] Some of the problems surrounding such an example can best be brought out by means of a variation on it.

Suppose there are two squirrels, both gathering nuts, who simultaneously walk out along two equally thin branches, one squirrel in the belief that the branch will not break or give way, the other squirrel without this belief: if their behaviour in walking out along the branches is the same, then how do we find out which squirrel has the belief that the branch will not break or give way? The only way I can see round this difficulty is to argue that their behaviour in walking out along the branches is *not* the same; one squirrel, the one with the belief, walks out along the branch, for example, more 'confidently' than the other squirrel. Assuming that what is referred to as confidence here can be empirically observed and can be observed to characterize the behaviour of only one of the two squirrels, the difficulty now is to understand how this correlation between belief and 'confident' behaviour has been arrived at by us in the first place. For in order to correlate 'confident' behaviour with belief, we should have somehow to penetrate to the squirrel's belief, examine it, and then observe that, when the squirrel had this belief, it walked out along the branch differently from when it did not have this belief. But we can never penetrate to the squirrel's 'belief' except, if at all, through its behaviour, which is all that we are directly acquainted with; how, then, are we supposed to find out in the first place that, when a squirrel walks out along the branch this way as opposed to that, it has the belief that the branch will not break or give way? Moreover, not even an inductive correlation seems possible, since we are in no position to affirm *either* that belief X is always followed by behaviour of type Y, since we can never get at the belief on its own, apart from behaviour, *or* that behaviour of type Y is always preceded by

[28] I owe this example to Paul Helm.

belief X, since we can never be sure, with only behaviour to go on, that *there is* a belief preceding (or even contemporaneous with) it. In the case of our two squirrels, then, the anti-Russellian faces a dilemma: if he allows that their behaviour in walking out along the branch is the same, then he is in no position to find out which squirrel believes the branch will not break or give way; whereas if he allows that their behaviour is different, and is right about this empirically, then he has no way of telling which squirrel's behaviour is the behaviour correlated with the belief that the branch will not break or give way.

The anti-Russellian can always protest, of course, that the example does not work for a different reason, namely, that if the behaviour of two squirrels in walking out along the branch is the same, then both squirrels have the belief that the branch will not break or give way. The trouble here is to understand just how the anti-Russellian knows this claim to be true.[29] If the claim is allegedly a synthetic truth, then I do not understand how the correlation of Y-type behaviour with belief X has come to be known and, much more importantly, has come to be known to hold *invariably*, such that behaviour of type Y by the squirrel *simply cannot occur* without the squirrel's having belief X. If, on the other hand, it is allegedly an analytic truth that both squirrels have the belief in question, then I think it must be the case either that the term 'belief' is being defined in terms of behaviour or that the concept of belief is being analysed in terms of behaviour; for it could not otherwise be analytically true that

---

[29] The anti-Russellian might try to do something here with the argument from analogy for other minds, in order to try to show that the squirrels have the belief in question. This argument has been fiercely attacked and is not well-regarded today. Indeed, it is widely condemned as a bad inductive argument, primarily because of doubts about the move from what is true in my own case to what is or must be true in the cases of others. I should have thought such doubts are bound to be especially acute when the argument is used to move from the human case to the case of our two squirrels, particularly in view of the obvious difficulty, which I have been emphasizing, of showing that the squirrels *actually have* the belief in question. Put differently, though one may use the argument to attribute a belief to our two squirrels, attributing a belief and showing they actually have the belief are two different things. For a recent discussion of the argument from analogy, see Alvin Plantinga, *God and Other Minds* (Cornell University Press, Ithaca, New York, 1967), Part III.

behaviour of type Y by a squirrel cannot occur in the absence of belief X. Whether it is the term or the concept that is being so treated, however, a 'détour' through the squirrel's supposed mind is 'wholly unnecessary'. (I return to the question of whether animals can have beliefs, and at some length, in each of the next two chapters.)

Here, then, are several reasons why the Russellian may persist in thinking that, though it is true that animals have wants in the sense of having needs, it is not true or at least cannot be known to be true, unless belief is treated behaviouristically, that animals have wants in the sense of having desires.

Though the position arrived at is not advanced by Russell in Lecture III of *The Analysis of Mind*, it is nevertheless Russellian in character, in that it remains completely faithful to his account of animal desire and the essence of desire; and, regarded as a supplement to and development of Russell, it renders his account of animal desire immune to the Kenny–Pears objection. For behaviour-cycles in animals *are* identified and individuated by means of wants as needs, and, what is the crucial addition, animals, unlike us, *cannot have* wants as desires. In the case of animals, in other words, there is nothing more than wants as needs to be accounted for, as there is something more to be accounted for in the case of conscious human desire. True, Russell's strict behaviourism is here modified; but the resultant position remains a form of behaviourism, I think, in virtue of the fact that (i) animals cannot have desires, (ii) needs, unlike desires, do not presuppose or make essential reference to minds, mental phenomena, beliefs, or consciousness on the part of those whose needs they are, and (iii) the relation between a need and the cycle of behaviour by which to still the need is a causal one.

Finally, so far as I can see, nothing in his position precludes the Russellian from allowing that animals — or, in any event, the 'higher' animals — are conscious.[30] His vital concern is to provide an account of what sets off behaviour-cycles in animals without having recourse to minds, mental

[30] Whether at the time of writing *The Analysis of Mind* Russell himself thought that animals were conscious, I am unsure; the influence of J.B. Watson upon Russell in this work, however, is profound, and Watson's animus towards all talk

phenomena, beliefs, or consciousness, and this he can do, whether or not and even if animals are conscious. This is particularly true, I think, since the ground of the Russellian's doubts about whether animals have desires consists in his reasons for doubting they have or can have beliefs, and his reasons for doubting that they have or can have beliefs do not consist in the supposition that they are not conscious.

---

of consciousness may well have infected Russell. It seems clear, in any event, that this particular animus has been instrumental in bringing about the recent demise of behaviourism; see, for example, B.D. MacKenzie, *Behaviourism and the Limits of Scientific Method* (Routledge & Kegan Paul, London, 1977), especially Chs. II and IV.

VII

Interests, Needs, Desires, and Beliefs

The question of whether animals possess interests turns fundamentally upon what analysis is given of the concept of an interest, and I want to make use of my remarks on this question in Chapters II and V, as well as my remarks on needs, desires, and beliefs in Chapters V and VI, in order to show that, however unlikely it may at first appear, on the traditional and most common analysis of interests, there is a strong case to be made in support of the view that animals do not have interests.

INTERESTS

Following Tom Regan,[1] we may distinguish between 'Good health is in John's interests' and 'John has an interest in good health'. The former is intimately bound up with having a good or well-being to which good health is conducive, so that we could just as easily have said 'Good health contributes to John's good or well-being', whereas the latter — 'John has an interest in good health' — is intimately bound up with wanting, with John's wanting good health. Now it is apparent that good health may be in John's interests, in the sense of contributing to his good or well-being, even if John does not want good health, indeed, even if John wants to continue to drink heavily, with the result that his health is irreparably damaged. It is equally apparent, however, that John may want to carry on drinking heavily, even if he comes to realize

[1] 'McCloskey On Why Animals Cannot Have Rights', 254; 'Feinberg On What Sorts Of Beings Can Have Rights', 487.

and to accept that hard drinking does not contribute to his over-all well-being. In other words, good health can be *in* John's interests without John's *having* an interest in it, and John can *have* an interest in hard drinking without its being *in* his interests. (Talk of 'having an interest' masks a distinction between 'having an interest' and 'taking an interest', which I shall return to and explain in Chapter XI; it is not relevant to our concerns here.)

Can animals — or, in any event, the 'higher' animals — have interests in either of these senses? If they can, then perhaps the minor premiss of Nelson's argument for the moral rights of animals can be sustained after all.

HAVING A GOOD

Do animals, therefore, have interests in the first sense, in the sense of having a good or well-being which can be harmed or benefited? The answer, I think, is that they certainly do have interests in this sense; after all, it is plainly not good for a dog to be fed certain types of food or to be deprived of a certain amount of warmth. This answer, however, is of little use to the Nelsonian cause; for it yields the counterintuitive result that even man-made/manufactured objects have interests, and, therefore, on the interest requirement or Nelson's major premiss, have or at least are candidates for having moral rights. There are several different ways of showing this.

(1) The applicability of the concept of 'not being good for' shows, I think, that that to which the concept is applied 'has a good', and this concept is straightforwardly applicable to objects. Just as it is not good for a dog to be deprived of a certain amount of warmth, so it is not good for prehistoric cave-drawings to be exposed to excessive amounts of carbon dioxide or for the paintings of Rembrandt to be exposed to excessive amounts of sunlight. But how could excessive amounts of carbon dioxide not be good for prehistoric cave-drawings unless those drawings had a good which they could fall away from and which excessive amounts of carbon dioxide made them fall away from? If, however, these drawings have a good, then, on the view presently under consideration, they have interests, and so have or are candidates for having moral rights.

(2) Consider the case of tractors: anything, including tractors, can have a good, a well-being, I submit, if it is the sort of thing which can be good of its kind;[2] and there are obviously good and bad tractors. A tractor which cannot perform certain tasks is not a good tractor, is not good of its kind; it falls short of those standards which tractors must meet in order to be good ones. Just as John is good of his kind (i.e. human being) only if he is in health, so tractors are good of their kind only if they are well-oiled. Thus, to say that it is in a tractor's interests to be well-oiled means only that it is conducive to the tractor's being a good one if it is well-oiled. Of course, farmers *have an interest* in their tractors being well-oiled; but this does not show that being well-oiled is not in a tractor's interest, in the sense of helping to make it good of its kind. It *may* show that what makes good tractors good depends upon the purposes for which *we* make them;[3] but the fact that we make them for certain purposes in no way shows that, once they are made, they cannot have a good of their own. Their good is being good of their kind, and being well-oiled is conducive to their being good of their kind and so, in this sense, in their interests. If this is right, if tractors do have interests, then on the interest requirement — that all and only beings which (can) have interests (can) have moral rights — tractors have or can have moral rights, and this is a counterintuitive result.

(3) It is tempting to object that tractors cannot be harmed and benefited and, therefore, cannot have interests. Consider again, however, the earlier examples: prehistoric cave-drawings are positively harmed by excessive amounts of carbon dioxide, and the paintings of Rembrandt are equally harmed through exposure to excessive amounts of sunlight. Both, but especially the former, begin physically to deteriorate under these conditions. It must be emphasized, moreover, that it is these objects themselves which are harmed, and that their owners (the nation, in the case of the cave-drawings) are harmed *only* in so far as and to the extent that the objects themselves undergo harm. Accordingly, on the

---

[2] I agree with Regan on this point and my discussion of it here and below parallels his; see his 'Feinberg On What Sorts Of Beings Can Have Rights', 492.
[3] Ibid. 493.

present objection, interests are present, and the interest requirement once again gives the result that objects or things have or can have moral rights.

To accommodate those who just might feel that objects or things can have moral rights, when these objects or things are, for example, significant works of art,[4] the example can be suitably altered, so that what is harmed is, for instance, a quite ordinary carpet. But if drawings, paintings, and carpets can be harmed, why not tractors? Surely a tractor is harmed by prolonged exposure to rain? And surely the harm the tractor's owner suffers comes through and is a function of the harm to the tractor itself?

(4) We determine goodness after their kind not only in the case of tractors and other man-made/manufactured objects but also, in an obvious sense, in the case of many animals. A sheep-dog is not good of its kind if it cannot collect sheep, and a pencil-sharpener is not good of its kind if it cannot sharpen pencils. We have bred and trained the one, designed and adapted the other, each to the performance of a task set by us, where success or failure in performing this task is also measured or determined by us; and even the standards by which we measure or determine success and failure in their tasks are themselves traceable to us. Of course, we vary the standards in dogs depending upon our purposes, so that, for example, the standards we put to lap-dogs are quite different from the standards we put to sheep-dogs; in both cases, however, it is we ourselves who draw up and apply the standards and determine success or failure in satisfying them, which is exactly what we do in the case of pencil-sharpeners. In short, these cases are alike in the role *we* play in devising, applying, and assessing the satisfaction of those standards which in each case determine goodness after their kind.

(5) It is tempting to object that only those things which can have needs, which can come to lack something in a vital respect, can have a good or well-being; and animals obviously have needs. The short answer to this, the most important objection, to which I return below, is simply that tractors

---

[4] See, for example, A. Tormey, 'Aesthetic Rights', *Journal of Aesthetics and Art Criticism*, xxxii (1973), 163–70; and D.A. Goldblatt, 'Do Works of Art Have Rights?', *Journal of Aesthetics and Art Criticism*, xxxv (1976), 69–77.

also have needs and, therefore, according to the objection it-self, a good; they can, for example, need oil. In a word, the mistake here is to assume that needs presuppose either consciousness or an awareness of the deficiency which con-stitutes the need, and neither of these is the case, as we saw in the last chapter.

In fine, it cannot be in this first sense of 'interest' that the case for animals and for the truth of Nelson's minor premiss is to be made; for though animals do have interests in this sense, so too do man-made/manufactured objects, with awkward results.

WANTS AND NEEDS

Do animals, therefore, have interests in the second sense, in the sense of having wants which can be satisfied or left un-satisfied? In this sense, of course, it appears at first blush that tractors do not have interests; for though being well-oiled may be a part of what it is for tractors to be good of their kind, tractors are not normally said to have an interest in being well-oiled, since they cannot want to be well-oiled. Farmers can have wants, however, and they certainly have an interest in their tractors being well-oiled.

What, then, about animals? Can they have wants? By 'wants' I understand a term which encompasses (at least) both needs and desires, and it is these which I shall consider.

At the end of Chapter V, I raised the prospect of some-one's trying to use a relationship between needs and interests in order to show that animals have interests, and I remarked then that we should have to block this route to a defence of the Nelsonian minor premiss. As the result of the discussion of needs in Chapter VI, it should now be apparent how this is to be done. If to ask whether animals can have wants is to ask whether they can have needs, then certainly animals can have wants. A dog can need water. But this *cannot* be the sense of 'want' upon which having interests will depend, since it does not exclude things from the class of want-holders. Just as cats and dogs need water in order to function normally, so tractors need oil in order to function normally; and just as cats and dogs will die unless their need for water is satisfied, so trees and grass and a wide variety of plants and shrubs will die unless their need for water is satisfied. It is perhaps worth stressing once again that, as the cases of tractors, trees, grass, shrubs, etc. show, needs do not presuppose or require consciousness and do not presuppose or require knowledge or awareness of the deficiency which makes up the need. If, in sum, we are to agree that tractors, trees, grass, shrubs, etc. do not have wants, and therefore interests, it cannot be the case that wants are to be construed as needs.

DESIRES AND BELIEFS

This, then, leaves desires, and the crucial question of whether animals can have wants as desires. We have already encountered one negative response to this question in the last chapter, viz. that of the defender of a Russellian behaviourism against the Kenny–Pears objection; but it is possible to think that animals cannot have desires even if one is not a behaviourist. In order to show this, I shall set out two additional arguments, one in this chapter and one in the next, neither of which involves assuming the truth of or in any way relying upon a Russellian behaviourism in respect of animal desire. Like the Russellian's position, however, these arguments do not require that we consider animals to be non-conscious; that is, the reasons they provide for denying desires to animals do not consist in or in any way involve the assumption that animals lack consciousness.

Before turning to the first of these additional arguments, a few general comments are necessary.

In denying that animals have desires, I am not denying something which ethologists, for example, are committed to regarding as vital to their work. For instance, none of the sophisticated behaviour-patterns of birds and other creatures which Niko Tinbergen discusses in his classic work *The Study of Instinct*[5] is traced to these creatures' desires or wishes; rather, he develops the concepts of instinct and innate behaviour responses (as well as that of learned behaviour

---

[5] N. Tinbergen, *The Study of Instinct* (Oxford University Press, Oxford, 1974). See also P. Marler, W.J. Hamilton, *Mechanics of Animal Behavior* (John Wiley & Sons, New York, 1966).

responses), neither of which requires the intervention of desires or wishes, in order to explain why these creatures behave as they do. In fact, explanations by means of what he calls 'subjective phenomena' are eschewed altogether by Tinbergen,[6] and if I have read Chapter One ('Ethology: The Objective Study of Behaviour') of *The Study of Instinct* correctly, such phenomena are considered by him to have no part whatever to play in how ethologists are to go about their business of understanding and explaining animal behaviour. He neither denies nor affirms the existence of desires, wishes, and hopes in animals; but he will have no part of what he calls 'guessing' as to an animal's subjective state,[7] as if such guesses were necessary in order to explain, for example, the rather stylized reproductive behaviour of sticklebacks or the intricate feeding behaviour of goldfish. And if guesses about the subjective states of members of our own species are risky, guesses about the subjective states of members of different species, and about how close such states in them resemble such states in us, are positively hazardous; certainly, they inject a totally alien element into the objective study of animal behaviour. (Significantly, Tinbergen does not rely upon the argument from analogy in order to endow members of other species with subjective states; and my remark about this argument in Chapter VI, note 29 — that one who relies upon it to endow an animal with this or that subjective state has no way of showing that the animal actually is in that state — indicates one good reason why it has no role to play in the objective study of animal behaviour. Nor does the oft-heard cry — 'the animal would not be behaving as it is unless it were in this or that subjective state' — receive any support whatever from Tinbergen's work; he does not so much refute this claim as ignore it.)

Yet, in the case of domesticated animals especially, many people, particularly lonely people, regard (and often want to regard) their pet as a kind of lesser human being, with a less rich but still plentiful mental life which explains why their cat or dog behaves as it does. Their pet loves them, they

---

[6] Op. cit. 2 ff. For an example of Tinbergen's method in action, see his *The Herring Gull's World* (Harper & Row, New York, 1972).

[7] *The Study of Instinct*, p. 5, also Ch. 6.

often say, and tries to be faithful to them, and they in turn try not to hurt its feelings (for example, by leaving it alone or ignoring it) and to return this deep affection. For understandable reasons, such people have nevertheless not been so rigorous as Tinbergen in divesting themselves of all traces of anthropomorphism in their attempts to understand and explain animal behaviour. It is as if the only way they can bring themselves to approach an understanding of their pet's behaviour is by first investing the animal with a human endowment and then finding as the explanation for why it behaves as it does precisely some feature of this endowment with which they have invested it. By describing the cat or dog and its behaviour in anthropomorphic terms and thereby 'putting' into the animal what one is going to cite as the explanation of its behaviour, there is no limit to the complexity and extent of the mental goings-on of cats and dogs, or rather the only limit is the range of mental life one is prepared to endow these creatures with in the first place, on some anthropomorphic paradigm. Indeed, the endowment now allegedly extends even to communication with animals by telepathy. The animal psychologist Beatrice Lydecker claims in her book *What the Animals Tell Me*[8] that one can, even though cats and dogs lack language, nevertheless communicate with and in this sense 'talk' to one's pet by means of something akin to ESP. One simply commands one's dog to sit and simultaneously forms a mental image of him in that position; and as this image is communicated to and received by him by telepathy, he will soon come to adopt the appropriate position. Doubtless to many the dog will be thought to be *like us* in being able to send and receive such images and to communicate in this way.

My objection is not to people endowing their pets on some paradigm with an extensive mental life *per se*; rather, it is to (i) citing some feature of this postulated endowment as the hard explanation for why their pet is behaving this way or that, when confirmation of this explanation is normally out of the question, and (ii) using some feature of this postulated endowment as a means of trying to squeeze animals into the class of right-holders. (And it is important to be aware that

[8] Harper & Row, New York, 1976.

even some positive accounts of moral rights depend upon ascribing animals human traits, in order to concede them rights. For example, rights, according to A. I. Melden's *Rights and Persons*,[9] are set and arise within a web of interlocking relationships among persons, and Melden is especially anxious to bring out and emphasize the multifarious aspects of these intricate and intimate relationships. He does not discuss the case of animals explicitly; but since he does not say that animals are persons (and very few of us indeed think otherwise), it would appear that they cannot possess moral rights. At a meeting of the American Philosophical Association in Washington (1978), Melden said, in respect of this implication, which I think he felt to be an unhappy one, that the more we ascribe human traits to animals the more inclined we will be to use the language of rights in respect of them. Why? Because, obviously, the more we can pile up the human traits we are prepared to endow animals with, the more likely we will be to regard them as honorary human beings or honorary persons and so to put them into a position to possess rights. So far as I can see, unless one is initially prepared to adopt a rather rampant anthropomorphism in respect of animals or else to fudge what one means by a 'human trait', pigs and chickens will continue not to be regarded as human beings or persons, in which case, on Melden's view, they can have no rights.)[10]

I turn now to the first of the additional arguments to show that animals cannot have desires. It is relatively complex, but only in the sense of having a number of different strands, which I shall set out in the remainder of this chapter. It consists in an analysis of desire and belief and of what it is to have beliefs; and it turns partially upon the view that having beliefs is not compatible with the absence of language.

Suppose I am a collector of rare books and desire to own a Gutenberg Bible: my desire to own this volume is to be traced to my belief that I do not now own such a work and

[9] Blackwell, Oxford, 1977.
[10] One might, of course, think up some analysis of what it is to be a person which did not consist in thinking of persons in terms of collections of *human* traits and which enabled pigs and chickens to be persons; but this ploy is not often resorted to by animal rightists.

that my collection is deficient in this regard. By 'to be traced' here, what I mean is this: if someone were to ask how my belief that my collection lacks a Gutenberg Bible is connected with my desire to own such a Bible, what better or more direct reply could be given than that, without this belief, I would not have this desire? For if I believed that my collection *did* contain a Gutenberg Bible and so was complete in this sense, then I would not desire such a Bible in order to make up what I now believe to be a notable deficiency in my collection. (Of course, I might desire to own more than one such Bible, but this contingency is not what is at issue here.)

Now what is it that I believe? I believe that my collection lacks a Gutenberg Bible; that is, I believe that the sentence 'My collection lacks a Gutenberg Bible' is true. In expressions of the form 'I believe that. . .', what follows the 'that' is a sentence, and what I believe is that that sentence is true. The same is the case with expressions of the form 'He believes that. . .'; what follows the 'that' is a sentence, and what the 'he' in question believes is that that sentence is true. The difficulty in the case of animals is this: if someone were to say, for example, 'The cat believes that the laces are tied', then that person is holding, as I see it, that the cat believes the sentence 'The laces are tied' to be true; and I can see no reason whatever for crediting the cat or any other creature which lacks language, including human infants, with regarding the sentence 'The laces are tied' as true.[11]

(This account of belief is in terms of sentences and not propositions. I adopt Quine's method in *Word and Object* for eliminating propositions in belief contexts in favour of sentences. Briefly, in 'John believes that the window is open', the sentence is no longer to be parsed as 'John believes/that the window is open'. 'Believes' is not, in other words, to be regarded as a term relating the name 'John' with the proposition named by 'that the window is open'. Rather, it is to be regarded as part of the operator 'believes that', an operator which, when applied to a sentence, says Quine, 'produces a

---

[11] Though the present argument may bear an affinity to arguments to be found in the work of Donald Davidson, it is not, so far as I know, his. I put the matter thus, because my argument here, though it did occur to me independently, nevertheless did so after listening to a discussion of Davidson. See below, n. 15.

composite absolute general term whereof the sentence is counted an immediate constituent'.[12] Put differently, the sentence is now to be parsed 'John believes that/the window is open', and 'the window is open' is a sentence and not a name at all and so not the name of a proposition. In this way, the suggestion that the sentence 'John believes that the window is open' expresses a relation between John and the proposition named by 'that the window is open' is removed. I should perhaps also remark that, though it may be thought that my analysis of belief requires persons to entertain the concept of a sentence in order to have beliefs, this in fact is not the case. Again, following Quine,[13] the sentence 'John believes that the window is open', if parsed as 'John believes that/the window is open', where 'the window is open' is not a name but a sentence, can be plausibly interpreted as 'John would, if asked, assent to some sentence that has for him the meaning that "the window is open" has for us', and what this amounts to saying, at least in part, is that John knows the use of a sentence which has for him the meaning that 'the window is open' has for us. This does not commit John to entertaining the concept of a sentence but it does commit him to knowing the use of a sentence, namely, a sentence which has for him the meaning that 'the window is open' has for us.[14])

Importantly, nothing whatever is affected in the case of the cat by changing the example, in order to rid it of sophisticated concepts like 'laces' and 'tied', which may in any event be thought to be beyond cats, and to put in their place more elementary concepts. For the essence of this argument is not about the relative sophistication of this or that concept but rather about what is believed. If what is believed is that a certain sentence is true, then no creature which lacks language can have beliefs; and without beliefs, a creature cannot have desires. Such is the case with animals, or so I suggest; and if I am right, not even in the sense of wants as desires, then, do animals have interests, which, to recall, is the minor

---

[12] *Word and Object* (MIT Press, Cambridge, Mass., 1967), p. 216.
[13] Ibid. 217.
[14] I am grateful to Jonathan Cohen for drawing these points to my attention and to Cohen and Paul Helm for helping me to deal with them.

premiss in the Nelsonian argument for the moral rights of animals.

BELIEFS AND LANGUAGE

But is what is believed that a certain sentence is true? It is, if I am right in what I maintain about the expressions 'I believe that. . .' and 'He believes that. . .'; and what I am maintaining is not unusual in the least. But there is a further argument which supports the claim that what is believed is that a certain sentence is true; it consists in simply thinking through my example of the Gutenberg Bible.[15]

(1) When I believe that my rare book collection lacks a Gutenberg Bible, I believe that it is true that my collection lacks a Gutenberg Bible; put another way, I believe that it is false that my collection contains a Gutenberg Bible. I can and do distinguish between the sentences 'My collection lacks a Gutenberg Bible' and 'My collection contains a Gutenberg Bible', and I cannot and do not regard both as true at one and the same time. That is, I do not believe that my collection both does and does not contain a Gutenberg Bible, do not believe that the sentences 'My collection lacks a Gutenberg Bible' and 'My collection contains a Gutenberg Bible' are both true. Rather, what I believe is that my collection lacks a Gutenberg Bible, that only one of these two sentences is true; and sentences *are* the sorts of things which I and others regard as capable of being true or false.

(2) Applying (1) to the case of the cat, I do not see how the cat can be correctly described as believing the laces are tied unless it can, as I do, distinguish between the beliefs that

---

[15] The argument which follows envelops Donald Davidson's claim ('Thought and Talk', in *Mind and Language,* ed. S. Guttenplan, Clarendon Press, Oxford, 1975, p. 22) that having beliefs requires the distinction between true and false belief. I owe my acquaintance with this claim to H.M. Robinson's pointing it out to me. I stress this, because I cannot pretend to be very familiar with Davidson's work in the philosophy of language and semantics (or, indeed, with these areas) and so am not really in any position to expound and develop parts of his work in my behalf. Thus, I cannot provide his defence of the above claim or say whether my defence of it — which turns upon our wanting to be able to say of the cat that it can be *correctly described* as believing the laces are tied — can receive support from his. So perhaps it would be best to say that my argument here contains an important Davidsonian plank or premiss; in any event, it owes him a debt.

the laces are tied and that the laces are untied and regards one but not the other as true. But what is true or false are not states of affairs which reflect or pertain to these beliefs; states of affairs are not true or false (though sentences describing them are) but either are or are not the case, either do or do not obtain. If, then, one is going to credit the cat with the belief that the laces are tied, and the cat, in order to be correctly described as believing this, must be able to distinguish this belief from the false belief that the laces are untied, and states of affairs are not true or false, then what exactly is it that cats are being credited with distinguishing as true or false? Reflection on this question, I think, forces one to credit cats with language, in order for there to be something true or false in belief; and it is precisely because cats lack language that we cannot make this move. Reflection on this question also forces us away from a reductionism of belief to behaviour in the case of animals (see the Russellian position set out in Chapter VI); for a reductionism appears incapable of showing a genuine distinction in the cat's case between the belief that the laces are tied and the false belief that the laces are untied, without which, as in our own case, it is difficult to see how the cat could be correctly described as believing the laces are tied. For if it cannot distinguish the belief that the laces are tied from the false belief that the laces are untied, what could it mean to say that the cat is to be *correctly described* as believing the laces are tied?

(3) I can and do distinguish, then, the sentence 'My collection contains a Gutenberg Bible' from the sentence 'My collection lacks a Gutenberg Bible', and only the latter do I regard as true. Now this sentence is true, obviously, only if my collection lacks a Gutenberg Bible; that is, the truth of what I believe here, that the sentence 'My collection lacks a Gutenberg Bible' is true, is at the very least partly a function of the actual state of my book collection. In other words, I not only regard the sentence 'My collection lacks a Gutenberg Bible' as true but I also am aware in doing so that the truth of this sentence is at least partly a function of my book collection actually being one way rather than another.

(4) In possessing a grasp of this relationship between the sentences 'My collection lacks a Gutenberg Bible' and 'My

collection contains a Gutenberg Bible' and the actual state of my book collection, I possess an awareness, to put the matter in the most general terms, of an intimate link between language and the world. I obviously do so, since I take the actual state of my book collection to be capable of showing the sentence 'My collection lacks a Gutenberg Bible', which I regard as true, to be false. However difficult to capture, a grasp of this link between language and the world is essential, if I am to be correctly described as believing that my collection lacks a Gutenberg Bible. For in order to be so described, I must grasp the difference between 'My collection lacks a Gutenberg Bible', which is the case, and 'My collection contains a Gutenberg Bible', which is not the case; and what makes one the case and the other not, what makes the former true and the latter false, is the actual state of my book collection.

(5) I can see no reason to credit a cat with an awareness or grasp of how language links up with the world; and I do not see how a creature *could* have such an awareness or grasp unless that creature was itself possessed of language. And cats are not possessed of language. In other words, then, if we are correctly to credit the cat with the belief that the laces are tied, we must endow it with language and with an awareness of a link between language and the world; and we cannot so endow it.

POSSESSION OF LANGUAGE

On the other hand, virtually no one to my knowledge has claimed that cats *are* possessed of language, perhaps because cats fall too far down the evolutionary scale. So let us ascend this scale to the rung immediately beneath us, arguably that of the chimpanzee, delve within the class of chimpanzees in order to single out the well-known case of Washoe, and ask whether Washoe is possessed of language.[16]

[16] Some interesting studies of 'language' and/or 'speech' in other chimpanzees are reasonably well-known. See, for example, C. Hayes, K.G. Hayes, 'Imitation in a Home-raised Chimpanzee', *Journal of Comparative and Physiological Psychology*, 45 (1952), 440–59; W.N. Kellogg, 'Communication and Learning in the Home Raised Chimpanzee', *Science*, 162 (1968), 423–7; and D. Premack, 'The Education of Sarah', *Psychology Today*, 4 (1970), 55–8. For a discussion of some of the general issues raised in work of this sort, see H.B. Sarles, 'The Study of

R. A. and B. T. Gardner[17] taught Washoe, a young female chimpanzee, a series of gestures known as American Sign Language. American Sign Language is comprised of visual gestures, normally called signs, which are made and shaped by the hands. Within Washoe's presence, this was the only form of communication used (there was, therefore, no attempt to get Washoe to reproduce human words vocally), and slowly, by repetition on the part of her teachers and by imitation on her own part, Washoe not only acquired but also mastered the use of numerous signs. By this, I do not mean merely that repetition and imitation were successful and that Washoe learned how to make different signs; I mean also that she conjoined signs and in ways that issued in conjunctions of signs which were themselves significant. For example, numerous conjunctions of two signs were made by Washoe, of the form 'gimme food' and 'me out', though the conjunctions made nearly always seem to have involved one of a range of signs found in the overwhelming majority of such conjunctions and a sign conjoined with one of these signs. In short, on the basis of Washoe's attainments in the use of American Sign Language, not merely in acquiring but also in conjoining (two and often more) signs, her case is said by the Gardners — so far as I am aware, correctly — to bear comparison with the cases of very young children and their acquisition, mastery, and use of two-word conjunctions.[18]

Language and Communication across Species', *Current Anthropology*, 10 (1969), 211–15; D. Premack, *Intelligence in Ape and Man* (Lawrence Erlbaum Associates, Hillsdale, N.J., 1976), particularly the later chapters; and W.H. Thorpe, *Animal Nature and Human Nature* (Methuen, London, 1974), especially Chs. 3 and 8. For a noteworthy discussion of the relation between human language and animal communication systems, which Chomsky attacks in Ch. 3 of *Language and Mind* (Harcourt, Brace & World, New York, 1968), see Thorpe's 'Animal Vocalization and Communication', in *Brain Mechanisms Underlying Speech and Language*, ed. F.L. Darley (Grune & Stratton, New York, 1967), pp. 2–10. For a series of discussions on animal communication systems, and on some of their similarities with and differences from human communication by means of language, see *How Animals Communicate*, ed. T. Sebeok (Indiana University Press, Indianapolis, 1977).

[17] R.A. Gardner, B.T. Gardner, 'Teaching Sign Language to a Chimpanzee', *Science*, 165 (1969), 664–72; 'Two-way Communication with an Infant Chimpanzee', in *Behavior of Non-Human Primates*, ed. A. Schrier, F. Stollnitz (Academic Press, New York, 1971), pp. 117–84.

[18] Of interest on this point is Roger Brown's 'The First Sentences of Child

Inevitably, then, the question arises of whether Washoe really is possessed of language, and it arises in circumstances where the case of Washoe is widely considered to be the best case yet in support of the view that an animal can possess language. I must warn the reader, however, that 'widely considered' here refers much more to popular accounts than, I suspect, to unanimity among primatologists. For example, some primatologists may well want to ascribe not language but language-like accomplishments to Washoe, in view of the limited range of her accomplishments as compared with those of even three-year-old children; more especially, however, others certainly do desire to see more work done on communicative processes generally before concluding that chimpanzees possess language. In this regard, work done at the Yerkes Regional Primate Center in Atlanta, Georgia,[19] is said to show that 'a final decision as to whether Lana (or any chimpanzee) does or does not have language cannot be made until a better understanding of the requisites for, and processes of, language is reached' and that, in order to obtain this better understanding, 'it is necessary to consider in further detail communicative processes in general'.[20] I do not mean to imply that the Yerkes primatologists are not strongly inclined to credit Lana with language, only that, as one might expect in scientific researchers, they are more careful about leaping to conclusions.

The answer to the question of whether Washoe is possessed of language depends upon what one takes the criterion of the possession of language to be, and philosophers and linguists often disagree on this among themselves; but to anyone who has been influenced by the work of Chomsky, it must be doubtful that Washoe is possessed of language, except in the most attenuated of senses. For the integrated whole of Chomsky's corpus — I have in mind especially, for our purposes here, *Aspects of the Theory of Syntax*,[21] *Cartesian*

and Chimpanzee', in *Psycholinguistics: Selected Papers,* ed. R. Brown (Free Press, New York, 1970), pp. 208-31.

[19] Summarized in *Language Learning by a Chimpanzee: The Lana Project,* ed. D.M. Rumbaugh (Academic Press, New York, 1977).

[20] E. Sue Savage, D.M. Rumbaugh, 'Communication, Language and Lana: A Perspective', in ibid. 288.

[21] MIT Press, Cambridge, Mass., 1965.

Linguistics,[22] and *Language and Mind* — supports a view of language as something entirely apart and distinct from animal behaviour. Without taking up an enormous number of pages and departing altogether from my narrative, it is impossible that I should review this already much-discussed corpus here; but one aspect of it I do want briefly to raise, since it generates a number of very important questions about Washoe's 'linguistic' *competence*.

A generative grammar is a set of lexical elements and rules on the basis of which the grammatically acceptable sentences of a language can be produced. In addition to lexical elements, a transformational generative grammar at the very least contains (i) a set of phrase-structure rules which determine the deep structure of the sentences of some language and (ii) a set of transformation rules for the production of actual surface structures in that language. The term 'grammar' here, then, refers both to lexical elements and to the over-all set of rules which provide the deep structure of the sentences of the language in question and which generate all the grammatically acceptable sentences of that language; and an important part of Chomsky's characterization of our command of language is that, given a finite number of lexical elements and a finite set of rules for producing sentences, we can produce and understand an indefinite number of sentences. The point is a vital one, both because it brings out our creative command of language and because it forms an integral part of what our linguistic competence consists in. The term 'competence' here, then, refers to a person's knowledge of the lexical elements and the over-all set of rules he has mastered so as to enable him not only to produce and understand an indefinite number of sentences but also to differentiate within the language grammatically acceptable sentences from those which are not, such as sentences containing grammatical mistakes, ambiguities, nonsense, etc. (Doubts perhaps arise as to the sense of 'know' in which a person can be said to know these rules — the allegedly explanatory notion of 'tacit knowledge' is not particularly illuminating — but the general characterization of linguistic 'competence' is at least

[22] Harper & Row, New York, 1966.

clear in outline.) Now the point is this: does Washoe display
such competence? Does she recognize mistakes? Does she
recognize ambiguities, and, for example, discard certain conjunctions because of this? Can she detect nonsense? In what
sense does she have a grasp of the syntactic categories of her
'language'.[23] Is the notion of her 'misapplying' the rules
which comprise her alleged competence a sensible one? In
what sense does she grasp these rules? Does she display the
creative command of language characteristic of us? Or is she
limited to a small number of 'meaningful utterances', depending upon what she has been taught, where the meaning
of any two signs in any two-sign conjunction is set for her
and where it is rarely, if at all, the case that she 'unfixes' a
sign's meaning and then uses the sign in new and significant
ways? And where she does allegedly 'unfix' a sign's meaning
and use it in a new way, to what extent is reinforcement
responsible for her using it in this way subsequently and to
what extent can accident, chance, etc. be discounted as the
explanation of her using that sign in the new way in the first
place? Indeed, is even speaking of 'unfixing' the meaning of
signs appropriate unless she has a grasp of the semantic
character of her 'language'? But in what sense does she have
such a grasp? A host of other questions about Washoe's

---

[23] Without some clear and demonstrable answer to this question, it is difficult to know how to assess the claim that some chimp or other can produce
novel sentences. For example, if on some occasion a chimp which has been conditioned to produce the sentence 'Give me some food' produces 'Some me give
food', does this count as a novel sentence? Or do the chimp's productions count
as novel only if they are grammatical *by our standards*? But then what if, as
Ernst von Glaserfeld reports of Lana ('The Yerkish Language and its Automatic
Parser', in *Language Learning by a Chimpanzee: The Lana Project*, p. 128), the
chimp's production of ungrammatical to grammatical strings of lexigrams (which
bear a one-to-one correlation with English words) is 80:70, 91:152, and 71:125
for 4-, 5-, and 6-lexigram strings? Even leaving aside the extremely important fact
that only grammatical strings are reinforced with food, does this show a grasp of
syntax and grammar? I am not clear that it does. (On a slightly different though
not unrelated point, if the chimp who produces 'I am sick' and 'Open the door'
on some occasion produces 'I am the door', does this count as a novel sentence
no matter what the context in which it is produced? I mean, is 'I am the door' a
novel sentence when it is inappropriately produced —say, in response to 'Do you
want banana?' — and when what is before the chimp is a banana and not a door?
In the above paper, von Glaserfeld counted productions of this sort as novel and
so included them as part of the data on which his statistics about Lana's novel
productions are based).

'linguistic' competence could be raised, but these suffice, I think, to indicate one of the important ways the work of Chomsky impinges directly on the question of whether she possesses language.

More generally, Chomsky's work argues forcibly against a view of language as an evolutionary development out of more simple communicative systems. That is, because language can be shown to be a human phenomenon, it is, he says, 'quite senseless to raise the problem of explaining the evolution of human language from more primitive systems of communication'.[24] The principles underlying animal communication systems are, he maintains, entirely different from those underlying human verbal behaviour; and though he does allow that such systems share 'many of the properties of human gestural systems' (importantly, the 'language' Washoe mastered was such a gestural system), the organizational principles underlying human language are beyond anything like those principles which are known to underlie gestural systems.[25] If Chomsky is correct, then, not only does language not grow out of or stem from behaviourally based systems of communication, with or without the addition of vocal sounds or signs, but language and animal communication systems are separated by a chasm which *no amount* of sophistication or complexity in animal behaviour can bridge. (I realize, of course, that this is a large question, on which much more can be said.)

I do not want to be taken to imply that arguments other than Chomsky's cannot be used in order to show that animals are not possessed of language; my point is merely that his work poses a sustained and systematic attempt to mark off language as a recognizably human development entirely distinct from animal behaviour and is for that reason, as ethologists such as R.A. Hinde[26] and W.H. Thorpe[27] have been quick to realise, much more striking and penetrating than any isolated argument one might employ to the same end.

[24] *Language and Mind*, p. 59.
[25] Ibid. 60 ff.
[26] *Non-Verbal Communication* (Cambridge University Press, Cambridge, 1972).
[27] *Animal Nature and Human Nature*, especially Chs. 3 and 8.

Nevertheless, two such isolated arguments are quite power-ful in their way and very much worth noting, not least be-cause they each have numerous adherents, as I know from the frequency with which I have encountered them in talking with others.

(1) Can Washoe lie? If not, why not? What these questions are getting at is this: if Washoe cannot lie, then she cannot assert anything; and if she cannot assert anything, she cannot be possessed of language. (And what of species lower down the evolutionary scale: can cats and dogs, cows and sheep lie?) On this argument, assertion is regarded as a *sine qua non* of the possession of language, and though it may be queried whether the essential or chief function of language is to assert, nevertheless it is the function with which philoso-phers, logicians, and others have most concerned themselves. Of course, the claim that Washoe does assert forces the argu-ment one stage backwards. Suppose Washoe makes a sign: does the very making of it amount to asserting? If so, then presumably Washoe never does anything but assert, such as ask a question, make a request, issue a warning, give an order, etc.; if not, then what is the nature of the addition which must be made to turn what Washoe does into asserting, and what is the specific difference between this addition and the addition which must be made to turn what Washoe does into asking or requesting or ordering?

(The claim that some chimpanzee or other *can* lie is in-creasingly to be met with in the popular press, though here too primatologists are usually more careful.[28] And caution is required. A mess is made by a chimp and its conditioner has observed it do so; the chimp is then asked, by sign or by means of a keyboard, whether it made the mess and it signals 'No' or presses the 'No' key. On the basis of this recurring, the chimp is held to have lied. But notice: a two-year-old child who said 'No' in similar circumstances to the chimp's would not be held to have lied even though it said 'No'. The point is that merely saying 'No' or making the 'No' sign does not show that either the child or the chimp knows what 'No' means, still less that it knows what lying is and is intentionally

[28] See, for example, D.M. Rumbaugh, T.V. Gill, 'Lana's Acquisition of Lan-guage Skills', in *Language Learning by a Chimpanzee: The Lana Project*, p. 185.

trying to deceive its conditioner or that it knows that using 'No' in certain types of contexts amounts to prevaricating. Moreover, it has been the case with every chimp which I have read about in the literature that reinforcement is used to bring about future production of a sign and lack of reinforcement to diminish future production of a sign. In other words, production of the 'No' sign diminishes, if it is not reinforced, whereas reinforcement of the 'No' sign brings about its future production. On the one hand, then, future production of the 'No' sign or lack thereof is accounted for by reinforcement, without having to hypothesize some desire in the chimp to prevaricate, even supposing it knows what that is. And if, after prolonged conditioning, the chimp still occasionally makes the 'No' sign in connection with the messes it makes, why is this evidence for the fact that it is lying as opposed to evidence for the fact that its conditioning is not yet completely successful, or, more straightforwardly, that it just does not grasp what 'No' means? On the other hand, should it be thought that it is the chimp's first use of the 'No' sign in this context which is the really significant one, assuming the chimp has not already been conditioned to produce it, then I do not readily see how accident, chance, etc. can be ruled out as the explanation for this.)

(2) There is a perfectly straightforward sense in which Washoe is a product of what she has imitated; and even if we concede her a limited inventiveness in devising variants of the signs she has been taught and using these variants in ways other than the old ones, and even if we concede her a limited inventiveness in conjoining signs this way and that, her basic 'linguistic' competence is of an altogether different order to that of all but very young children. I want to stress this, if only to provide some perspective to the achievements of Washoe, Lana, and the others. This in no way diminishes their achievements or the achievements of those primatologists who have experimented with them. But the fact is, for example, that Lana has, through long and painstaking conditioning, been brought to a level of 'linguistic' competence in Yerkish — a computer-based, language-type system of signs displayed on a keyboard in which what can be communicated (often to do with food) is already a minute

percentage of what can be communicated in a natural language and in which the mode of communication has been radically simplified — that is comparable only to that of very young children. To be plain, the linguistic attainments of quite ordinary children of thirty to thirty-six months far exceed those of Washoe, Lana, and other chimpanzees,[29] and beyond this age, all bases of comparison in these attainments have vanished entirely. Now this leads to an obvious observation: the more we push the criterion for the possession of language in the direction of the linguistic competence of articulate human beings, the less likely we are to consider Washoe possessed of language, whereas the more we push the criterion in the direction of the linguistic competence (or lack thereof) of very young children the more likely we are to consider Washoe possessed of language. Now why should we adopt the latter course? That is, why should we not follow the ordinary man in holding that very young children *are not* possessed of language but, if anything, are in a learning situation with respect to language? If one then wants to say the same of Washoe, why can we not go on to point out that, *unlike* very young children, Washoe never progresses sufficiently beyond these very early learning situations to enable us to say that she, too, is at last possessed of language? This view still enables us to compare the achievements of Washoe to those of very young children; but it incorporates a dynamic view of linguistic growth and makes possession of language turn upon the outcome of undergoing such growth, which Washoe never undergoes. Some such view as this, for example, almost certainly underlies S. Zuckerman's somewhat harsh remark that 'the day someone teaches two chimpanzees a conceptual language, and then records their conversations — as opposed to getting the animals to respond to, or even repeat, human sounds or signs — I shall sit up and take notice'.[30] One *can* push the criterion for the possession of language in the direction of the 'linguistic' competence of very young children, just as one *can*, as we saw in connection with the argument from

[29] I do not mean to imply, of course, that primatologists mask this fact or in some way overlook it.
[30] *From Apes to Warlords* (Hamish Hamilton, London, 1978), p. 72.

marginal cases, lower the requirement for the possession of rationality to some absolutely minimal level; but the truth is that we do not really regard very young children either as rational or as possessed of language, and we all know that one pretends otherwise, or moves in the direction of such pretence, usually because one has some particular axe to grind.

CONCLUSION

I conclude, then, that a strong case can be made for the view that animals do not have desires and can be made in a way which neither assumes the truth of nor relies upon a Russellian behaviourism in respect of animal desire. This in turn enables me to reach the additional, more basic conclusion that the Nelsonian minor premiss — that animals have interests — is doubtful at best, at least on the traditional, most common analysis of interests. For animals either have interests in a sense which allows things and man-made/manufactured objects to have interests, and so, on the interest requirement, to have or to be candidates for having moral rights, or they do not have interests at all, and so, on the interest requirement, do not have and are not candidates for having moral rights.

VIII

Simple Desires and Self-Consciousness

The second of the additional arguments to show that there is a strong case to be made for the view that animals cannot have desires has its roots in a quite specific objection to the discussion of desire contained in Chapters V, VI, and VII. I hinted at this objection in Chapter VI, when I deferred consideration of a possible attempt by the anti-Russellian to distinguish different kinds of desires and to hold that, though animals may not be able to have all kinds, nevertheless they can have some kinds. I want now to take up this objection, give it substance, and then show how it can be met.

As I have found through several discussions, when the previous chapter was read in the form of a paper, the critic who suggests that there are different kinds of desires and that I have at best only shown that animals cannot have certain kinds almost certainly has in mind a particular class of desires which I have overlooked, a class which someone who analyses desire in terms of belief may seem likely or even bound to overlook. Specifically, this critic is likely to have in mind that, however many kinds of desires there are, there is a class of desires — let us call them 'simple desires' — which do not involve the intervention of belief in order to have them, and which do not require that we credit animals with language. The claim that there are such desires is not a new one, and Aristotle's discussion of them in Books II–VI of the *Nicomachean Ethics* is as useful as any.[1]

---

[1] Trans. W.D. Ross (Clarendon Press, Oxford, 1925). The account of Aristotle which follows is indebted to N.J.H. Dent's excellent article, 'Varieties of Desire', *Proceedings of the Aristotelian Society, Supplementary Volume*, 1 (1976), 153–

Though adult human beings can and do occasionally act impulsively, we are not simply driven or moved to act by impulses, drives, and instinctive reactions. In this, for Aristotle, we differ from animals and very young children. That is, unlike them, we have the capacity to ponder, weigh, and choose what we will do. It is as if, in fact, the acts which alone bear the complete and total imprint of our nature are those which we have chosen or deliberately willed; and the desire upon which choice and deliberation is dependent is *boulesis* or 'wish', which carries overtones of reasoning. In the case of animals (and very young children), on the other hand, their behaviour has its genesis in desire as *epithumia* or 'appetite', which does not carry any such overtones. In essence, Aristotle's account of animal behaviour is this: by means of their senses, animals detect things which come within their purview; this sensory detection sets off or activates a pleasing or painful reaction in them; and the release of this reaction in behaviour ensues. What form that behaviour takes depends upon whether the reaction activated is pleasing or painful to the animal: if pleasing, the animal is, as it were, enticed by that which it has sensed; if painful, it is repelled by what it has sensed. Accordingly, when my dog spies his supper, a pleasurable reaction is set off or induced in him, and he goes forward to his evening meal. He does not first ponder the wisdom of stoking up in view of his impending evening romp. Nor does he first argue with himself thus: easting keeps up my strength; that meat and cereal will enable me to eat; therefore, I had better go and eat it. Rather, he is straightforwardly impelled to act by the reaction activated in him by seeing and/or smelling his food. It is true, of course, that eating enables him to romp and keep up his strength; but he does not operate with any notion or idea or belief in these respects and so argue and draw the conclusion that he had better go and eat his meat and cereal.

Aristotle's account, then, is, I think, essentially behaviouristic in character, not totally unlike what we have encountered

---

75. To anyone interested in developing and then fleshing out a concept of simple desire, Dent's article is of great assistance. Dent's co-symposiast, John Benson, provides a useful critique of and supplement to Dent's views: ibid. 177–92.

already in the case of Russell. In my dog's case, the stimulus is his seeing and/or smelling his food, which engenders or activates a pleasing reaction in him; and this reaction issues in his going over and consuming his evening meal. Now the important point about a stimulus–response account of behaviour, whether in the case of Russell or Aristotle or anyone, is this: there is nothing required to 'fit between' an activated reaction and its issuance in behaviour. Thus, in the case of my dog, nothing is required to mediate between the pleasing reaction activated in him by spying his supper and his behaviour of dashing over and eating. And if nothing is required to mediate between an activated reaction and behaviour, then there is no room in which to insert ideas or thoughts or beliefs, whether about the wisdom of his stoking up for this evening or keeping his strength up or whatever. In other words, as we saw in the case of the Russellian, my dog behaves as he does without my having to attribute, say, beliefs to him, in order to explain why he behaves this way. He simply has an inherent propensity to behave one way when a pleasing reaction is activated in him and to behave another way when a painful reaction is activated in him. Accordingly, one might come to say of my dog that he 'desires' the food, without requiring in the least any beliefs or the possession of language on his part.

On the basis of this or a similar account,[2] then, it may be suggested that there is a class of desires — 'simple desires' — which do not involve the intervention of belief, in order to have them, and which do not require that we credit animals with language. Such simple desires, for example, may be for some object or other, and we as language-users might try to capture these simple desires in the case of my dog by describing its behaviour in such terms as 'The dog simply desires the food' or 'The dog simply desires the bone'. The vital point is this: if all my dog's desires are simple desires, then the arguments of previous chapters to show that dogs lack beliefs, in order to show that they lack desires, may well be beside the point, since in order to have simple desires neither

---

[2] Obviously, a similar account need not be similar in respect of being a stimulus–response account; it need only be similar in leaving no room for belief (and/or language) in the having of simple desires.

belief nor language is necessary on the part of the dog.

What is needed, therefore, is an argument to cover this possibility. Suppose, then, my dog simply desires the bone: is it aware that it has this simple desire? It either is not so aware or it is, and I will consider each possibility in turn.

(1) *The dog simply desires the bone but is unaware that it simply desires the bone.* It may be thought that there is nothing so very odd in this, in allowing the dog to desire without being aware that it desires; but it seems to me to raise a problem of a difficult order. In the case of human beings, unconscious desire can be made sense of, but only because we first make sense of conscious desire; where no desires are conscious ones, however, where the creature in question is alleged to have only unconscious desires, what cash value can the use of the term 'desire' have?[3]

The point of this question can be brought out another way. On the strength of its behaviour alone, it is alleged that the dog simply desires the bone; the desire claimed for it is one which, if it has it, it is unaware that it has; and no distinction between conscious and unconscious desire is to be drawn in the dog's case, since all the dog's desires are simple ones, which, on the present claim, it is unaware that it has. Consider, then, the case of a plant which, through a series of movements which can be documented and recorded, shuns the dark and seeks the light: by parity of reasoning with the dog's case, we can endow the plant with an unconscious desire for a place in the sun, and claim as we do so that it, too, is something for which no distinction between conscious and unconscious desire is possible. In other words, without an awareness condition of some sort, it would appear, especially given the intricacy, for example, of plant[4]

---

[3] One might want to draw a distinction here; that is, one might want to say of us that we *become aware* of our conscious desires, in order to leave room for our presently having conscious desires of which we are unaware. Accordingly, why not say of the dog that its simple desires are conscious desires of which it is unaware? In these terms, my point would be that, where a creature is said never to become aware of its desires, as in the case of the dog, it would then have to be and to remain unaware of all of its conscious desires, in which case I do not know what it would mean to say of that creature that it had 'conscious desires'. (I am grateful to Peter Singer for discussion on this point.)

[4] Cf. P. Tompkins, C. Bird, *The Secret Life of Plants.*

and insect[5] life, that the world can be populated with an enormous number of unconscious desires in this way; and it no longer remains clear what, if anything, the cash value of the term 'desire' is in such cases.

The point, then, is that the dog must be aware of at least some of its simple desires, if the term 'desire' is not to be drained of all significance.

(2) *The dog simply desires the bone and is aware that it simply desires the bone.* On this alternative, if the dog is aware that it has this simple desire, then it is aware that it simply desires the bone; it is, in other words, self-conscious. My objections to conceding self-consciousness to the dog are twofold.

First, I adhere to the view that language is necessary in order to possess self-consciousness; and dogs lack language. The view that self-consciousness requires language is, of course, not new with me, and my own views on the subject are very close to those expounded at length in Chapters VIII and IX of P.M.S. Hacker's *Insight and Illusion.*[6] Perhaps a much-truncated argument for the view here, however, will suffice to indicate the line of thought behind it. Following Kant's 'Refutation of Idealism', I adopt the views that inner, subjective experience presupposes outer experience and that experience of objects in outer sense is a *sine qua non* condition for the possession of self-consciousness.[7] Following Chapter III ('Persons') of P.F. Strawson's *Individuals*, I adopt the view that 'P-predicates', which include such things as thoughts, feelings, memories, and perceptions, can only be ascribed to oneself if they can be ascribed to others and that one can know one has or experiences a particular P-predicate R only if one can know that other people have or experience R.[8] And following Wittgenstein's private language argument, I adopt the view that P-predicate R, for example 'pain', does not (and cannot) have meaning by standing for or naming a

[5] See especially E.O. Wilson's absorbing work, *The Insect Societies* (Harvard University Press, Cambridge, Mass., 1974).

[6] Clarendon Press, Oxford, 1972, pp. 215–82. I came to my views on this subject as the result of discussing these pages of his book with Peter Hacker.

[7] *Critique of Pure Reason*, trans. N. Kemp Smith (Macmillan, London, 1970), 'Postulates of Empirical Thought', B274–9.

[8] Methuen, London, 1964, pp. 87–116.

sensation to which each of us has access in his own case but rather has meaning in virtue of certain public rules and conventions which can be adhered to and transgressed, where adherence and transgression can be publicly checked.[9] In this way, I come with Hacker to the view that the meaningful ascription of P-predicate R to oneself is only possible if one can meaningfully ascribe it to others and that one can meaningfully ascribe it to others only within the context and confines of a public language. In other words, if one cannot meaningfully ascribe thoughts, feelings, memories, etc. to oneself except within a public language, then one has a ground for holding that self-consciousness presupposes the meaningful ascription of P-predicates to others within a public language.[10]

Second, and equally important, there is nothing in either my or my dog's behavioural repertoire by which we can indicate the possession of self-consciousness.[11] Consider memories: with language, I can not only ascribe memories to myself, but I can as well indicate that I am presently having a memory of something, am presently remembering. But in response to the question 'What are you thinking about?', I can not only reply that I am remembering my first meal at Maxim's but I can also indicate that I am presently aware of remembering this meal; and my remembering and my awareness of remembering I can equally well capture and reveal in language. Were I to lack language, however, I should be forced to reveal not only my remembering but also my awareness of remembering this meal at Maxim's in my behaviour, and there is no act or set of acts I could perform which would reveal this.[12] Importantly, this is not because

---

[9] *Philosophical Investigations,* ed. G.E.M. Anscombe, R. Rhees, trans. G.E.M. Anscombe (Blackwell, Oxford, 1953), Sections 243 ff.

[10] I am aware, of course, that much more can be said on this subject, particularly in respect of Wittgenstein's private language argument, on which Hacker's book is very thorough indeed.

[11] My discussion here owes a debt to Peter Singer and Peter Hacker.

[12] A similar point is made by Anthony Kenny in *Will, Freedom and Power* (Blackwell, Oxford, 1975), p. 5. I am grateful to Paul Helm for bringing this passage to my attention. I regret this volume did not come to my notice in time to consider it in this book, since Kenny appears at first glance often to reach conclusions in respect of animals contrary to mine. But he certainly does accept that animals are not self-conscious.

of any deficiency in me, but because there is no act or set of acts or pattern of behaviour which is that of being aware of remembering, whether in men or animals, just as there is none for being aware of being sad or being aware of being happy. *The reason* there is no act or set of acts or pattern of behaviour which is that of being aware of remembering or being sad or happy is that no piece of behaviour constitutes being aware *vis-à-vis* remembering or being sad or happy. In other words, I can remember and I can be aware that I am remembering; but nothing in my behavioural repertoire constitutes being aware, such that, by doing it as well as something else, I can convey my awareness of remembering as opposed to my remembering. Whatever I do is consistent with just remembering.

The case of my dog is similar but worse: he has no way of conveying by means of his behaviour that he is aware of desiring the bone and, therefore, that he is aware of having this simple desire; but in my dog's case, it *could only* be on the basis of his behaviour that he *could possibly* be credited with an awareness of a simple desire in the first place. Two conclusions can, therefore, be drawn. First, since my dog cannot convey being aware of desiring the bone in his behaviour, we have lost the only basis we had for ascribing him simple desires. Second, since overt behaviour is all that virtually all animals present us, and since it is only on the basis of that behaviour that they *can possibly* convey their possession of simple desires, and since that behaviour cannot convey the awareness condition insisted on under the present interpretation of simple desires, I think we can reach the further conclusion that overt, physical behaviour, *however complex or complicated,* will never suffice to endow animals with simple desires under an awareness condition. For complexity and complication in behaviour is compatible with lack of awareness of the complexity and complication and, therefore, with the lack of a simple desire. Taken out of the context of simple desires, I do not agree that complex, complicated behaviour patterns suffice to endow animals with self-awareness; for either those very patterns are consistent with the absence of an awareness condition or it must be shown, not assumed, that behavioural indices of such a condition are provided either in the precise nature of the complexity and complication involved or in some feature of the behaviour to which the precise complexity and complication are related. This is no way denies, of course, that such complex, complicated behaviour occurs; but it does indicate that I am most reluctant to accept an argument of the form 'The animal would not be behaving in the complicated way it is unless it were aware of what it was doing'.

Even, then, if we concede for the sake of argument that there is a class of simple desires, desires which do not involve the intervention of belief and/or language in order to have them, the suggestion that we can credit animals with these desires, especially the suggestion that we can do so without having to credit them with language, is problematic at best. We have here, therefore, a second, additional argument for the view that animals cannot have desires; and it, too, does not assume or rely upon a Russellian behaviourism in respect of animal desire. Like our other arguments in this regard, however, the reasons it provides for denying (simple) desires to animals neither consist in nor involve the assumption that animals lack consciousness.

What I have suggested in this chapter is that animals lack self-consciousness and so a concept of self, to which all their subjective experiences are (to be) ascribed. To maintain this is not, however, to maintain a thesis which, as one person in discussion put it, 'even a greater fool could see was mistaken'. When I put a bowl of *WONDERCHUNKS* in front of my car, nothing happens; when I put a bowl of *WONDERCHUNKS* in front of my dog, a frightful scene ensues. As everyone accepts, my dog but not my car reacts, perhaps, it must be said, impulsively, perhaps in the vice of his drives and instincts; but he reacts. And the very fact that he reacts so emphatically at the appearance of his meals suffices, I think, to dispel any doubts about whether he is conscious. To continue to doubt that he is conscious when he reacts to *WONDERCHUNKS* in that way is possible, I think, only if one is very, very securely in the grip of a theory; and I do not think I am. My dog lacks desires, beliefs, and language in my view, but he is conscious; and because he is conscious, he can suffer unpleasant sensations (see Chapter XI). But though he is conscious, he lacks a concept of self, to which his subjective experiences are ascribed; and, as I have made plain, I agree with Hacker that he could not have such a concept, unless he were blessed with language. My view,[13] then, is not that which it has often been taken to be in discussion and which Singer, Regan, Clark, and others blast in their work; I am not suggesting that, because they lack language, animals can be factory farmed without suffering. Animals *can* suffer, which they could not unless they were conscious; so they are conscious. Nothing I have said in earlier chapters and nothing I will say in subsequent chapters is intended to deny this fact, which animal rightists correctly insist upon. But animals lack that reflective awareness which enables us to see our experiences and acts as our own (and thereby, of course, unlike animals, to be responsible for our acts).

Finally, these remarks bear upon Michael Tooley's widely influential discussion of the right to life in his paper 'Abortion and Infanticide'.[14] Since I am only using Tooley's view to show one implication of the arguments of this chapter, I shall not develop it but merely present his own summary of it. It comes to this:

> To sum up, my argument has been that having a right to life presupposes that one is capable of desiring to continue existing as a subject of experiences and other mental states. This in turn presupposes both that one has the concept of such a continuing entity and that one believes that one is oneself such an entity. So an entity that lacks such a consciousness of itself as a continuing subject of mental states does not have a right to life.[15]

If the arguments of this chapter succeed, animals lack a concept of self and have nothing in their behavioural repertoire by which to indicate the possession of self-consciousness, with, therefore, on Tooley's analysis, obvious implications for their right to life.

Of course, Tooley's requirement in order to have a right to life — that a creature have a concept of itself as a continuing subject of experiences and believe itself to be such a subject —

[13] It is Kenny's as well: *Will Freedom and Power*, p. 5.
[14] *Philosophy and Public Affairs*, 2 (1972), 37–65.
[15] Ibid. 49.

is a relatively severe one,[16] and animal rightists are as a result not very likely to be enamoured of it anyway, whatever the effect of my arguments. After all, not even the most ardent lover of my dog, however carefully he observed its enthusiasm for *WONDERCHUNKS* and for burying and digging up old bones, would find it easy to make out that it satisfied Tooley's requirement.

[16] For example, as Michael Martin points out, in addition to most animals, Tooley's requirement is almost certain to deprive human infants and severely mentally-enfeebled human beings of a right to life; see Martin's 'A Critique of Moral Vegetarianism', *Reason Papers No. 4* (Fall 1976), 31.

IX

Belief, Behaviour, and the Argument from Perception

In the last chapter, we were concerned with a critic who wanted to attribute desires to animals without having also to attribute beliefs and/or language to them; but there is also to be considered the critic who, in spite of earlier arguments, wants still to attribute beliefs to animals and so in this way to meet my demands in respect of their having desires. To this critic I now want to address several additional arguments.

THE INTELLIGIBILITY OF BELIEF-ATTRIBUTIONS

On the basis of their behaviour, we say that 'The dog believes that there is a bone buried in the backyard' and that 'The cat believes that the ball is stuck'. (We do not often say even these things of many animals, including food animals, in whose behaviour we do not, as it were, 'see ourselves'.) Most people, I suppose, assume such sentences as these to be straightforwardly intelligible and, indeed, true, given the animal's behaviour is of the appropriate sort. Quite apart from my earlier remarks to show that animals lack beliefs, however, there are reasons for thinking the intelligibility of such sentences is not quite the open-and-shut affair it is made out to be; and one of these reasons focuses attention upon an important problem, which I shall pursue in the subsequent section.

If we are to attribute beliefs to animals, then how are we accurately to capture the content of their beliefs? When we say 'The cat believes that the ball is stuck', do we really wish to maintain that the cat possesses *our* concepts of 'ball' and 'stuck'? Plainly not. But if the cat lacks our concepts of 'ball' and 'stuck', what does it mean to say that 'The cat believes that the ball is stuck'?

In Chapter II of *Belief, Truth and Knowledge*, D.M. Armstrong confronts this problem and suggests what is perhaps the best-known way of trying to deal with it.[1] This is to treat 'believe that' expressions used of animals as referentially transparent constructions, so that, 'in saying that the dog believes that his master is at the door we are, or should be, attributing to the dog a belief whose exact content we do not know but which can be obtained by substituting *salva veritate* in the proposition "That his master is at the door".'[2] Armstrong thinks that this way of proceeding 'shows that we need not give up our natural inclination to attribute beliefs to animals just because the descriptions we give of the beliefs almost certainly do not fit the beliefs' actual content'.[3] Two points are worth noting about Armstrong's contention. First, our critic who thought the sentence 'The cat believes that the ball is stuck' was intelligible almost certainly did not think it intelligible along the lines Armstrong is suggesting. What *he* thought was that he was accurately capturing what the cat believed when he said it believed that the ball was stuck. Put differently, to this critic, one does not capture the content of the cat's belief by substituting the equivalents in feline concepts for our concepts 'ball' and 'stuck'; for, most importantly, he does not know what these feline concepts are and how they differ from our own, is in any case not sure that there are any such specifically feline concepts or quite how he would go about establishing that there were, and does not take himself to be maintaining something very subtle in connection with them when he says 'The cat believes that the ball is stuck'. In short, I think he will agree that, in effect, Armstrong tries to save the intelligibility of the sentence 'The cat believes that the ball is stuck' by construing it as saying that the cat believes something or other, though we cannot say quite what. Second, how can we substitute *salva veritate* in the expression 'that the ball is stuck', unless there is a notion which the cat possesses which refers to the

[1] D.M. Armstrong, *Belief, Truth and Knowledge* (Cambridge University Press, Cambridge, 1973), pp. 24–7.   [2] Ibid. 26.   [3] Ibid. 27.

same object referred to in this expression by 'ball'? Armstrong makes it appear as if the only question here is one of what this notion is. It cannot, for example, be *our* notions of 'physical object' or 'material object' or 'independent thing' or 'substantial entity within my visual field', since it is highly doubtful the cat possesses these; we are left, therefore, with feline concepts, though without any idea as to what these are and how they are formed. Appearances, however, are sometimes deceiving, and so they prove to be in this case. For there is certainly a prior question to the one Armstrong pursues, namely, how do we know the cat *possesses* a notion which refers to what 'ball' refers to? We are only going to wonder what this notion is if we think the cat possesses such a notion in the first place, and the claim of possession obviously requires argumentation. You will not convince me that the cat has a feline concept which refers to what 'ball' refers to, however, just because it presses its nose against the ball, rears up and scratches it, and miaows. My old headmaster's cat did the same to the school's fire-extinguishers, my bicycle, its own reflection in the mirror, and the shadow cast on a wall by a wooden bird on a weather-vane, and I do not think I am alone in doubting whether cats have concepts of these. Seen another way, if the cat's behaviour is compatible with ascribing it a concept of ball, then that exact same behaviour is compatible with ascribing it any number of other concepts whatever, which yields, in addition to the problem of how we differentiate all these concepts, the bizarre conclusion that the very same limited behavioural repertoire suffices to endow animals with countless numbers of concepts, including, it would seem, some highly complex ones.

I shall not pursue this issue of intelligibility further. Enough has been said to indicate why, if we cannot say what it is the cat believes, the intelligibility of sentences ascribing beliefs to the cat may come to be regarded as compromised.

BEHAVIOUR AND PROPOSITIONS

I pass now to another argument in support of the view that animals cannot have beliefs. My argument here is addressed to those who, like Armstrong, either analyse belief propositionally or at least allow it to have propositional content;

and this includes, I suspect, a vast number of philosophers.[4] In any event, there is a point here of the utmost importance to the issue of whether animals have beliefs.

Armstrong's way of interpreting 'believe that' clauses used of animals is an attempt to maintain the intelligibility of our attributions of beliefs to animals in the face of a difficult objection; but it does not show, as he is aware, that animals *have* any beliefs. That is, on the strength of the dog's behaviour we say, with Armstrong, 'The dog believes that his master is at the door'; but our attributing this belief to the dog is not the same thing as showing that it actually has this belief. What we require, if we are to move from describing the dog's behaviour in our own terms as 'believes *that p*' to holding that the dog actually has the belief *that p*, is some account of the connection, not between behaviour and our attributions of belief, but between behaviour and having beliefs. Now if, as Armstrong, one allows belief to have any propositional content whatever, even propositional content that is to be regarded as referentially transparent; and if, as Armstrong, one is prepared to concede that dogs do not possess language; then it must be the case, if one is going to claim that dogs actually do have beliefs, both that they have some grasp of this propositional content and that behaviour alone can suffice to show that they have such a grasp. It is the latter, fundamental point I suspect, and I have two arguments to support the view that it is doubtful that behaviour alone *can show* that my dog grasps the belief *that p* or the propositional content of the belief *that p*.

(1) I do not understand how behaviour can *show* that my dog possesses the belief *that p* unless that behaviour is connected with the belief *that p* in such a way that that same piece of behaviour is not compatible with the belief *that q* or *that r* or *that s*. For if the dog's behaviour is compatible both

---

[4] Because I am here addressing Armstrong and others who analyse belief propositionally or at least allow it to have propositional content, I shall allow myself in this section to speak of the belief *that p*, where *that p* is a proposition. I remind the reader, however, that I follow Quine in eliminating propositions in belief contexts in favour of sentences; see above, Ch. VII. What I say here is consistent with what I say there, since in each instance where I speak of belief in terms of propositions here, I would resort to the method set out there to eliminate them in favour of sentences.

with the belief *that p* and with these other beliefs, then I do not understand how it can be concluded on the basis of that behaviour that it is the belief *that p* which the dog has, that it is the propositional content of the particular belief *that p* of which the dog has a grasp. For example, several months ago, my dog wagged its tail furiously when its master was at the door but also when its lunch was about to be served and when the sun was being eclipsed by the moon. On all three occasions, it barked and jumped about. So far as I could see, its behaviour was the same on the last two occasions as it was on the first, and I am not at all clear how, on the basis of that behaviour, it can be concluded that it was the belief that its master was at the door which the dog had, that it was a grasp of the propositional content of *this* belief and not some other which the dog had. (This point finds its analogue, in respect of the possession of concepts, in the earlier example of my old headmaster's cat.)

Of course, it can always be maintained that there *were* publicly observable differences in the dog's behaviour from one occasion to the next, if only I had been very careful in conducting my observations. But this possibility is rapidly reduced to an implausibility, depending upon how far it is taken. For the number of different, individual beliefs attributed to dogs would fill tomes, and it is simply implausible to contend that there is always a nice difference in their behaviour from one occasion of attribution to the next. It is implausible, because, if other dogs are like my dog, the behavioural repertoire of dogs is itself limited; and wagging its tail, barking and jumping back and forth comprise a large part of this repertoire.

In short, if there is no behavioural ground for distinguishing my dog's alleged grasp of the belief *that p* from its grasp of other beliefs, we acquire a ground for calling into question its alleged grasp of this belief in the first place. Or, seen the other way round, so long as my dog wags his tail, barks, and jumps about, we can credit him with a grasp of (the propositional content of) countless beliefs. Either way, the cutting edge to the dog's behaviour, in order to force us to concede it beliefs, is lost, since one and the same ground concedes the dog either no beliefs at all or any number of beliefs whatever.

(2) I do not understand how a piece of behaviour could be connected with the belief *that p* in such a way that we could conclude on the basis of the presence of that piece of behaviour that my dog actually had the belief *that p* or had actually grasped the propositional content of the belief *that p* unless it were the case that there were some intrinsic or internal connection between that piece of behaviour and the proposition *that p* itself.[5] The reason is this: the dog allegedly believes *that p*; according to Armstrong, *that p* is, even if in a referentially transparent fashion, what is believed; *that p* is a proposition;[6] and the dog's behaviour alone must suffice to show that it grasps this proposition *that p*. But if its behaviour is in fact to show that it grasps just this particular proposition, just this proposition *that p*, then surely there must be some intrinsic or internal connection between that behaviour and that proposition? Otherwise, we could never tell from its behaviour just which proposition the dog had grasped, that it was the proposition *that p* and not the proposition *that q* which the dog had grasped. But there is no such connection between the dog's wagging its tail, barking, and jumping about and the proposition 'Its master is at the door', since that behaviour is equally compatible with the propositions 'Lunch is about to be served' and 'The sun is being eclipsed by the moon'. In sum, by persistently depicting the dog's behaviour as believing *that p* or believing *that q*, we can portray it as believing all sorts of things; but its behaviour could not show that it grasped the propositional content of the particular belief *that p* unless that behaviour and that proposition were connected in ways which they are not.

It does no good to invoke the notion of behaviour as a criterion for belief. It is agreed on all sides that the dog's behaviour is the criterion used for attributing beliefs to it; what is at issue now, given that belief is analysed propositionally or allowed to have propositional content, is whether the dog's behaviour alone can suffice to show that it has grasped

---

[5] I agree with Bernard Harrison on this point; see his Critical Notice of Jonathan Bennett's *Linguistic Behaviour*, *Mind*, lxxxvi (1977), 603.
[6] See above, n. 4.

a proposition. I am suggesting that it cannot; but whether it can or cannot, the notion of behaviour as a criterion for the *attribution* of belief is not to the point.

I do not accept, therefore, that my dog grasps propositions, as Armstrong's analysis of belief demands that he do if he is to have any beliefs at all. One can, of course, so water down the term 'proposition' that the mere fact that all female robins sit upon their eggs — without, I might add, having been taught to do so — shows that they have all grasped some very elementary proposition, but a proposition nevertheless, about the survival of their species. Even this seems to me exceedingly implausible; but, more importantly, I am not clear, here as earlier, *why we should prefer* this type of explanation to one making reference to some innate behavioural response, particularly when the evidence for the latter is altogether stronger than the evidence for the former. (Indeed, is there any evidence for the former? So far as I can see, the only reason here for trying to endow animals with a grasp of propositions is that Armstrong's analysis of belief is in these terms and so demands, if animals are to have any beliefs, that they grasp propositions; and from this point it is but a short step to watering down either the term 'proposition' or the term 'grasps', in order to make the claim that animals grasp propositions and so have beliefs plausible.) Even on a watered down version of what a proposition is, in other words, I can see no reason for simply conceding, in the absence of argument, that animals grasp propositions and so, on Armstrong's analysis, the propositional content of beliefs.

Put succinctly, then, my argument against Armstrong and animal beliefs here is this: if belief is analysed propositionally or allowed to have propositional content, and if my dog is to have any beliefs, then it must be shown that my dog grasps the proposition *that p* or the propositional content of the belief *that p*; if this is to be shown, given my dog lacks language, then it must be the case that my dog's behaviour alone suffices to establish such a grasp; since it is doubtful, however, that behaviour alone can suffice to show that my dog possesses this grasp, it must be doubtful that we can conclude *on the strength of its behaviour*, which is all we have to go on, that my dog actually has some beliefs.

THE ARGUMENT FROM PERCEPTION

Finally, I think we can bring these discussions of intelligibility and animal behaviour to bear upon another reasonably well-known argument by which it is hoped to endow animals with beliefs. The argument, as given by Armstrong,[7] is straightforward enough, though any full discussion of it would be difficult without a good deal of empirical information. It is this: if the cat perceives that p is the case, then the cat knows that p is the case; and if the cat knows that p is the case, then the cat believes that p is the case. Each of these entailments, especially the second, has frequently been challenged; but I shall not repeat these arguments here. Instead, I want to raise three other considerations, which rely in part upon some themes of Kant, as found in the *Critique of Pure Reason*.[8]

(1) Suppose someone says, 'The cat believes that the ball is stuck', and bases this claim upon the (alleged) fact that the cat perceives that the ball is stuck: I am only going to allow that the cat has this belief if I allow that the cat perceives that the ball is stuck; but, following Kant, I am only going to allow that the cat perceives that the ball is stuck if it possesses the concepts requisite in order to have such a perception, namely, to take but two, the concepts of 'ball' and 'stuck'. There is here, then, a point about intelligibility — how can the cat believe that the ball is stuck unless it possesses the concepts 'ball' and 'stuck'? — and a point about perception — how can the cat perceive that the ball is stuck unless it possesses the requisite concepts of 'ball' and 'stuck'? — to be distinguished.

(2) Consider the point about perception: it will be replied that, nevertheless, the cat perceives something or other as evidenced by its behaviour. But behaviour alone will not show *what* the cat perceives, that is, what categories of things it recognizes and therefore, so to speak, the categorial terms in which its experience is presented to it; and if we do not

[7] *Belief, Truth and Knowledge*, p. 27.
[8] 'Preface', 'Introduction', and the 'Transcendental Aesthetic', together with the 'Transcendental Deduction'. The discussion of Kant which follows, as all my other discussions of Kant elsewhere, owes a debt to my former teacher P.L. Heath, whose course on Kant's epistemology remains for me a model of all philosophy courses should be.

know what the cat perceives, we cannot on the present argument know what the cat believes.

(3) Still, the cat does perceive, it will be replied, so the argument at least shows *that* the cat believes something or other, even if we cannot say *what* it is which the cat believes. Following Kant again, however, I do not think we can affirm *tout court* that the cat does perceive, that, in other words, we can separate in this artifical way perceiving from the categorization of what is perceived. What I mean is this: perception involves not only sensory detection but also comprehension by the mind. Essentially, 'comprehension by the mind' here means nothing more for Kant than subsuming particulars under universals, subsuming and thereby classifying the data of sense under concepts. The judgement 'This is an acorn' does precisely that, by subsuming and classifying a part of the sensory manifold by means of the concept 'acorn'. Now making sense of the sensory manifold in this way, such as has occurred at a more general level with 'I perceive that the acorn is green', is an exercise in judgement. A judgement for Kant is exactly what it was for Aristotle: it consists of a predicate and a subject, and making judgements involves attaching a (more general) predicate to a (less general) subject, as in 'This is an acorn' and 'Most acorns are green'.

Furthermore, when I say 'This is an acorn', I use the concept 'acorn' in order to make this judgement, and the judgement amounts to saying that what I have detected by means of the senses is judged by me to be acorn. What is presented by the senses are bits of colour, bits of taste, etc.; but, by means of concepts, these bits of sensory data are comprehended by me as a such-and-such. In other words, a judgement like 'This is an acorn' interprets the manifold of sense, which does not come pre-interpreted or pre-comprehended but rather in the form of Humean impressions; and perception refers to the sensory manifold interpreted, not purely and simply to the sensory manifold and to the bits of colour, taste, etc. which comprise it. I could go on filling in this view, but its Kantian character should by now be familiar.

My point is this: perception, for Kant, involves judgement, since what it is to use concepts, even *a priori* concepts, is simply to make judgements by means of them; and making judgements consists in attaching concepts or predicates to particulars or subjects. This view has three immediate implications for the case of animals. First, animals can only have perceptions if they can make judgements, and they can only make judgements if they can attach predicates to subjects. It is at the very least not obvious that they can do this; indeed, given their absence of language, it may well seem obvious that they cannot. Second, I cannot see or hear my dog attaching predicates to subjects, not because *my* dog happens to have a limited behavioural repertoire and deficient or abnormal instincts, but because wagging its tail, barking, and jumping about do not count either as conceptualization or as attaching predicates to subjects, in dogs or any other creature. Third, one cannot, as the present line of argument would, separate judgement from perception, since in the absence of the comprehension of sensory data by means of concepts, though the data of sense remains, having this data does not amount to having perceptions. That is, merely from having sensory data, which cats and dogs assuredly have, it does not follow that they have perceptions; and, on the present argument, it only follows that animals believe that p if they perceive that p.

The result of these three considerations, therefore, is to provide grounds, if not for rejecting, then at least for doubting the success of the argument from perception in endowing animals with beliefs. And this result, together with those on the intelligibility of belief-attributions and on behaviour and the propositional content of beliefs, reinforces the view of preceding chapters that, at least on the traditional, most common analysis of interests, animals do not have interests.

X

Emotions, Reasons, and Rational Desires

Analyses of the concept of an interest, other than the one I have been considering, can doubtless be thought up, and it may be that one or more of these can be made to yield the result that animals have interests.[1] I shall not, however, pursue this matter. Instead, I want in this chapter to exhibit certain upshots of the views I have been arguing for other than the ones I have already set out. My aim here is certainly not that of pronouncing definitively on the three issues I shall raise; rather, it is the altogether more modest aim of showing how the earlier arguments of this book provide us with a *plausible, defensible* position on each of these issues.

EMOTIONS

It is arguable that, though perhaps not all desires are based on

[1] Some important work on the concept, in which the analysis is in terms of rational choice, has recently been done in political theory. See I.D. Balbus, 'The Concept of Interest in Marxian and Pluralist Analysis', *Politics and Society*, i (1971), 151-77; W.E. Connolly, 'On "Interests" in Politics', *Politics and Society*, ii (1972), 459-77; and Grenville Wall, 'The Concept of Interest in Politics', *Politics and Society*, v (1975), 487-510. Relevant here also are Brian Barry's 'The Public Interest', in *The Bias of Pluralism*, ed. W.E. Connolly (Atherton Press, New York, 1969); and Virginia Held's *The Public Interest and Individual Interests* (Basic Books, New York, 1970). I very much doubt that animals can make rational choices, at least on any fruitful interpretation of that expression, which standardly involves a cost/benefit assessment of the probable, future consequences of different, hypothetical courses of action.

Some interesting classificatory work on the concept of an interest, in respect of demarcating the boundaries of expressions such as 'have an interest' and 'take an interest', has recently been done by A.R. White in 'Dewey's Theory of Interest', in *John Dewey Reconsidered*, ed. R.S. Peters (Routledge & Kegan Paul, London, 1977), pp. 35-55. I take up the distinction between having an interest and taking an interest in Ch. XI.

emotions, some may be, so that, if animals can have emotions, it might just be the case that they can have some desires after all. I doubt, however, that animals can have emotions, and my argument to support this claim turns fundamentally upon the fact that they do not have beliefs.

Emotion, as I see it, involves more than one integral component in its analysis; and among these integral components, at least in the case of a good many emotions, figures the notion of belief. Consider shame: in order to be ashamed, it is not enough that I slink about or feel unease or pangs of self-loathing; I must also think or believe that I have made a fool of myself, or have made myself look ridiculous in the eyes of others, or have committed a *faux pas*, or have transgressed the canons of good conduct, or so on. Of course, if I am ashamed of myself, I doubtless will slink about and suffer pangs of disquiet and self-loathing; but I would not be ashamed of myself unless I believed that I had discredited myself in some way. In short, I think the analysis of shame involves a number of items, among which is the thought or belief that I have in some way discredited myself, as a result of which, usually, I suffer a diminution in self-esteem.

Now this view of the emotions, obviously, is not new with me; indeed, especially since the appearance of Kenny's *Action, Emotion and Will*, I think it may fairly be described as forming the ruling view of the emotions today. It finds perhaps its earliest home in Book II of Aristotle's *Rhetoric*,[2] which W.W. Fortenbaugh has recently considered in detail in his *Aristotle on Emotion*;[3] and, as Fortenbaugh has pointed out, it denies animals emotions.

Aristotle argues that belief is a part of, if not all, then at least a good many emotions, including fear and anger, which

---

[2] In *The Basic Works of Aristotle*, ed. R. McKeon, trans. W.R. Roberts (Random House, New York, 1966).

[3] W.W. Fortenbaugh, *Aristotle on Emotion* (Duckworth, London, 1975). My account here of the *Rhetoric*, and, indeed, my account of the emotions generally, has been influenced by this exceptionally clear and compact work, in which the thesis that animals do not have emotions is also embraced. I am grateful to A.C. Lloyd for drawing this illuminating work to my attention and for discussing his very useful review of it (in *Archiv für Geschichte der Philosophie*, 58 (1976), 268-71) with me. Possibly neither man would accept my Kantian view of judgement, either in what follows or in my earlier comments on the matter in Ch. IX, though each agrees that the emotions involve judgement.

are the emotions most often regarded by us to be ones which animals can have. Thus, anger is said to involve a belief of outrage because of slight; fear, a belief of danger or harm; hate, a belief of someone as falling within a particular class, such as liar or thief; pity, a belief of undeserved suffering; and so on. The point is not that Aristotle regards the emotions as either wholly consisting in or wholly exhausted by beliefs, only that such beliefs are a part, and a necessary part, of them. If this is right, and it *is* a widely held position, then animals can only have emotions if they can have beliefs; and if I am right in my contention that animals do not have beliefs, then it follows that they cannot have, if not all, then at least a good many emotions.

Five observations can be appended to this conclusion in order to help flesh it out and to provide an account of several of the features of emotions which are commonly noted today.

(1) In order to be ashamed, I have to think or believe that I have made a fool of myself or have appeared ridiculous in the eyes of others or have committed a *faux pas* or whatever; for convenience, I shall say that I have to think or believe that I have discredited myself in some way. Importantly, however, what I think or believe does not have to be true; even if I am mistaken, and I have not discredited myself, it is nevertheless my believing that I have which accounts for why I am ashamed. In order to be ashamed, in other words, beliefs about discrediting oneself can be false, a point which, as we shall see below, is also the case with many of our moral feelings.

(2) If I am ashamed of myself, it is because I believe I have discredited myself; it is I myself who I believe to have brought discredit upon myself, and it is I, accordingly, of whom I am ashamed. Likewise, when I am ashamed of my vicar for his pinching of the actress's bottom, it is because I believe he discredits both himself and what he stands for; it is because of what I believe about him that it is *he* of whom I am ashamed. If emotional verbs take intensional objects, as is now, since Kenny's book, commonly accepted, it is because of the presence of beliefs as part of the emotions.

(3) I am ashamed of the vicar because I believe he pinched the actress's bottom and thereby discredited himself; but I

was rather far away at the time, preoccupied with his sizeable wife, and you now inform me that you saw the whole episode and that he merely brushed up against the actress. If I do not accept what you say, for whatever reason, then I will continue to believe that the vicar discredited himself and so continue to be ashamed of him; put differently, so long as I do not accept what you say, I can continue to accept that the vicar, so to speak, merits my shame, for what I believe he did. But if I do accept what you say, continued shame of the vicar is out of place and unmerited by anything he did; I cannot continue to accept that the vicar merits shame as a bottom-pincher if I no longer believe that he is one. In short, if we can argue about and so affect people's emotional reactions,[4] it is because those reactions are not of the stimulus–response variety but rather are grounded in beliefs; and by attacking or defending, supporting or contradicting the relevant beliefs in which people's emotions are grounded, I can in many cases argue and ease them out of their particular emotional reactions.

(But not in all cases: there are some deviant, though, to my mind, parasitic cases.[5] For example, some people do have an irrational fear of dirt, out of which they cannot be argued. This is because their fear is not based upon any true or false belief, for example, about their personal health, which is doubtless why we think of their fear as 'irrational'. Again, a number of people cannot bring themselves to enter an aeroplane, even though one explain carefully to them the statistics which show flying to be the safest form of travel; for this reason, we think of their fear of flying as irrational. Such deviant, 'irrational' cases exist, but an understanding of them is possible, I think, only because we can stand back and contrast them with normal cases, where belief is present.)

(4) In order to be ashamed, I have said that I have to think or believe that I have discredited myself in some way, and it has been suggested to me[6] that some people may try to insert a gap between thought and belief here. For example, if having

---

[4] See, e.g., Fortenbaugh, op. cit. 30.

[5] I am grateful to Vernon Pratt for impressing cases of this sort upon me and discussing them with me.

[6] By A.C Lloyd.

images counts as thinking (I shall not contest this, though my Kantian leanings lead me to deny it), and if animals can have images, then perhaps they can be said to have in some form the thoughts requisite for having emotions, even if it is the case that having images is not the same thing as having beliefs. But this line of reply does not impinge on my argument here, and for a reason linked to my discussion in the last chapter of Kant on judgement.

The emotions, as Fortenbaugh has argued, involve judgement.[7] But how? The answer, I think, in respect of shame, for example, is that one has to judge what was said or done to have been discrediting, that unless one so judges one will not believe one has discredited oneself. In my example in the last chapter of the cat and perception, I said that perception for Kant requires judgement; the judgement 'This is an acorn' classifies a part of the sensory manifold by means of the concept 'acorn'. As a result of making this judgement, I for Kant come to believe that I perceive an acorn; I do not first believe I perceive the acorn and then come to make the judgement that I do. In other words, there is, I think, a connection in Kant between judging this to be an acorn and believing this to be an acorn. Likewise, by extension, I think there is a connection between judging what I said or did to have discredited myself and believing I have discredited myself: if I judge what I did to have been utterly ridiculous and foolish, I form the belief that I have discredited myself, and this belief in turn produces shame in me. Even if what I believe turns out to be false and my judgement mistaken, as it often does, I have nevertheless accounted for why I am presently ashamed of myself.[8]

Thus, to say only that shame involves a belief on my part of having discredited myself is to leave out the important Kantian feature of how I have come to form this belief;

[7] Op. cit. 26 ff.

[8] Something of a similar view is taken by R.C. Solomon in his paper 'The Logic of Emotion', *Noûs*, 11 (1977), 41-9. Certainly, the Kantianism in my view is also present in Solomon. But whereas Solomon wants to argue that emotions are judgements (admittedly, of many different sorts), I want to stick to the more minimal view that they involve judgements (and, therefore, beliefs and the use of concepts). Solomon also provides a good, succinct account of earlier views of the emotions as well.

when we add, therefore, my judging that I have brought discredit upon myself, we can see the entire chain of requirements extending before us. Now I do not see how judging what I did to have discredited me can consist in an image; and even if we allow what was done to be captured in an image, and for an animal to have images, the image still requires judgement in order to be construed as an image of discrediting oneself or of making oneself ridiculous or foolish. So the claim that animals can have images does not affect my case.

(5) In order to be ashamed, I have to believe that I have discredited myself in some way, which in turn requires me to judge what I said or did to have discredited me. If earlier arguments in this book are correct, animals do not have beliefs and cannot form judgements. A further reason, Kantian in character, why animals cannot form judgements should now be apparent. For how can one judge oneself to have discredited oneself unless one possesses the requisite concepts, since, to take but a single concept, to judge that one has discredited oneself classifies or categorizes what was done by means of that concept? Hence, if animals lack that concept, they cannot judge themselves to have been discredited, which in turn means they do not believe that they have been discredited, which they must do in order to be ashamed. So, either animals cannot be ashamed or one is forced to begin speaking again of, for example, canine or feline concepts of discrediting oneself or looking the fool or appearing ridiculous; and the reader already has before him my reasons for lack of sympathy with canine and feline concepts.

The reason my dog is never ashamed, then, is that he lacks the concepts, judgements, and beliefs necessary in order to be so. This is not to say that he cannot behave in this way or that; but it is to say that he lacks the concepts by which to judge and cannot judge behaving in these ways to be discrediting himself and so cannot come to believe himself to have been discredited, which he must do in order to be ashamed. (What I say here of shame I should say of the other emotions as well.)

Finally, and on a different note, it is apparent that shame, pity, love, hate, fear, anger, etc. figure prominently in our moral psychology, so that, by trying to deny animals a share in these emotions, I seem implicitly to be depriving them of a moral psychology at all.[9] I accept this implication; and I suggest further, outside the context of Aristotle and Kant, that animals are deprived of a share as well in what we ordinarily think of as *moral feelings*. This is because belief is presupposed in order even to possess many of these feelings. Thus, it by no means follows that those who are guilty must or do feel guilty. What in my view is required to make this connection is the concept of belief. One feels guilty only when one comes to believe that one did wrong; and even if this belief is false, even if one is not guilty because one has not done wrong, one can nevertheless feel guilty because one believes one has. Again, compunction, the feeling of having to make something up to someone, would seem to turn entirely upon one's belief that one has done them an injury, whether or not one has in fact done so. And remorse would appear to hinge upon our now believing, whatever we believed in the past, that what we did was wrong, whether or not it actually was. It is an important facet of our moral psychology that even false beliefs can give rise to some of these feelings; but the reason my dog never feels guilt or compunction or remorse, justifiably or otherwise, is because he has no beliefs, true or false. I shall not argue the matter further. My point is simply this: without beliefs, my dog is denied desires, emotions, and a good many, if not all, moral feelings; and without these, it is hard to see what sense could be attached to crediting him with a moral psychology at all.

REASONS

If animals lack beliefs (and desires and emotions), then they cannot have reasons for actions. I suspect that the claim that animals cannot have reasons for actions will be *relatively* uncontroversial; so any controversy which surrounds this claim

---

[9] Fortenbaugh speaks of animals being denied a share in moral virtue, op. cit., Ch. 4. I am not certain how extensive the phrase 'moral virtue' is either in Fortenbaugh or Aristotle; but my claim here about animals lacking a moral psychology reflects my view, as will be seen, that animals lack the desires, emotions, and moral feelings which comprise a large part of a human being's moral outlook.

is most likely to centre not upon the claim itself but upon my manner of supporting it. My argument in support of it is as follows: to act for a reason either is or involves acting on a belief; animals do not have beliefs; therefore, they cannot act for reasons. The reader already has before him my case for the truth of the minor premiss of this argument; quite naturally, therefore, his attention is bound to focus upon the major premiss, and it is this which I want very briefly to consider.

A good place to begin is with the account of my dog and his meal as I gave it in Chapter VIII, in connection with the discussion of simple desires. When I put his evening meal before him, my dog detects it; his detection activates or sets off a pleasing reaction in him; and this reaction issues in his going and consuming his meat and cereal. He does not argue with himself about the wisdom of keeping up his strength or the necessity of stoking up in view of his impending romp this evening and so conclude that he had better go and eat. Nor does he have to be ascribed any beliefs in these respects. His detecting his food simply activates a pleasing reaction in him; and this reaction, unless dominated by a more intense one, will, if he is not troubled with indigestion or down with an attack of the colic, issue in his racing off to his supper. Accordingly, nothing is required to 'fit between' his reaction and his behaviour, with the result that there is no place for belief to be inserted into the account; my dog simply has an inherent propensity to behave this way or that, depending upon whether the reaction set off in him is pleasing or painful.

Now given this story, my dog plainly does not do what he does for a reason.[10] And so long as there is no opening or interval between his activated reactions and his behaviour, he *cannot* have reasons for action. For stimulus–response behaviour is typically the very antithesis of an agent doing what he does for a reason. The point, however, is not confined merely to stimulus–response accounts of the dog's behaviour; for unless some account of his behaviour can be given, such that *there is* an opening or interval between his activated reactions and his behaviour, there will simply be no

---

[10] This is Dent's view as well; see 'Varieties of Desire', 169.

room for reasons for action. For though it is true that my dog would not dash off to his supper unless he detected it when I filled his dish, this fact alone will not show that his detection of the food *serves him as a reason* for dashing off. Nor will appeal to the pleasing character of the reaction he has show otherwise, since the mere fact that the reaction is pleasing will not show that its pleasing or hedonic tone *serves him as a reason* for dashing over to his supper. In both of these cases, his doing what he does is consistent with his lacking reasons.

This talk of *serving him as a reason*, however, is critically ambiguous; and light can be shed on how it is to be unpacked by means of two, commonly received distinctions which the above account of the dog enables us to make. First, when my dog dashes off to his meat and cereal, he acts reasonably but not for a reason.[11] He acts reasonably because his needs, just as ours, press in upon him, and they must be satisfied if he is to keep going; and eating his supper helps him to keep going. Meat and cereal keep him going, but it is not because he believes this that he scampers off to his meal, so that this belief *serves him as a reason* for eating his meat and cereal; his needs and the behaviour which they set off require, as we saw in the case of the Russellian, no beliefs on his part whatever. Second, I may say of my dog, as I watch him consuming his meat and cereal, that wholesome food, regularly administered, keeps his strength up and that this very fact is *a* reason for his eating his supper; but this is not at all to say that this fact *serves him as a reason*, in the sense of being *his* reason for going and eating his supper. The latter is about the dog's reasons, about what Don Locke calls agent-reasons,[12] whereas the former is in essence merely a different way of saying that eating his meat and cereal of an evening keeps him going; and the former can be and remain true even though the latter is not.

Why does not the fact that eating his meat and cereal keeps him going, therefore, serve my dog as his reason for consuming

---

[11] Ibid. 168 ff.

[12] D. Locke, 'Reasons, Wants, and Causes', *American Philosophical Quarterly*, 11 (1974), 169–79. I accept Locke's account of agent-reasons, as will be evident in what follows.

his evening meal? The answer, I think, doubtless with a good many other people, is simply that, though consuming his supper will in the nature of things keep him going for another day and enable him later to set out on his nightly romp, he does not believe that this is so and, therefore, use this belief as a ground for action. (Nor will I accept, for reasons given earlier, that his consuming his supper simply shows that he has this belief.) Thus, lacking beliefs, a belief in the present regard cannot serve him as a ground or reason for doing what he does; he does what he does without any beliefs whatever, and, hence, without grounds or reasons for what he does.

The point can be illustrated in human terms, by a recent newspaper story. It appears that more and more people are moving out of Liverpool because of the high crime rate in the inner city, and nearly everyone interviewed by a local reporter agreed not only that the high incidence of crime was a reason but also that it was a good reason for moving away. But it never becomes an agent-reason for *my* moving away unless I believe there is a high incidence of crime in the inner city. Likewise, consuming his meat and cereal of an evening keeps my dog going and enables him to take his evening romp; but this never becomes an agent-reason for his consuming his supper except through his believing, for example, that his consuming his supper keeps him going, enables him to step out in the evenings, etc. If, however, dogs do not have beliefs, then even if we allow *a* reason to be facts of this sort, it cannot be concluded therefrom that they serve dogs as grounds or reasons, as agent-reasons for actions.

Finally, the fact that dogs lack beliefs proves significant in another way; for, as Locke notes,[13] agent-reasons are typically either beliefs or such things as desires and emotional states. I have already argued, however, that desire and emotion are partially to be analysed in terms of belief; the second of these classes, therefore, ultimately reduces to the first, in which case, if dogs lack beliefs, they cannot have agent-reasons for action.

---

[13] Ibid. 169 f.

RATIONAL DESIRES

Any and all utilitarians require a principle of utility. In the case of act-utilitarians, it will be applied directly to individual acts, whereas in the case of, for example, rule-utilitarians, it will be applied to individual rules (or sets of rules), whether conventional or otherwise. At present, however, in spite of the recent surge of interest in utilitarianism, and in act-utilitarianism in particular, there is no characterization of the principle considered free of difficulties; certainly, there is no accepted characterization. No small part of the problem here has been the inability of utilitarians to agree even among themselves upon what is to be understood by 'utility'.

Some explanation of 'utility' is obviously required; otherwise, the injunction expressed in and by the principle of utility itself cannot be carried out. For example, left unexplained, the principle of utility might be characterized in such terms as 'Always maximize net utility';[14] but this very characterization brings out its own shortcoming, namely, that without some explanation of what we are to take 'utility' to be, we shall have no idea of what it is we are supposed to be trying to maximize. How, then, is 'utility' to be understood? I want to draw attention to several consequences vis-à-vis animals on this score.

One of the most significant developments in recent work on utilitarianism has been the shift away from interpreting utility in terms of the possession of certain cognitive states or states of mind, collectively called 'pleasure', 'happiness', and so forth, and interpreting it instead in terms of the satisfaction of interests.[15] R. M. Hare, J. Griffin, J. Narveson, and others have objected that to confine utility merely to a concern with states of mind is too narrow and that the notion should either be expanded to include or else be defined in terms of the satisfaction of interests. (I do not mean to imply

---

[14] Something along these lines is suggested by Kai Nielsen in his 'Some Puzzles About Formulating Utilitarianism', *Ratio*, xv (1973), 256–62.

[15] For a useful discussion of this shift, see J.J.C. Smart, 'Hedonistic and Ideal Utilitarianism'. Of interest here also, because it brings in the case of animals in respect of this shift, is R.B. Brandt's 'The Psychology of Benevolence and Its Implications for Philosophy', *Journal of Philosophy*, lxxiii (1976), especially pp. 445 ff.

that there is not a rearguard action, especially by act-utilitarians, to resist this shift; there is. I mean only to imply that the shift represents an important, and, I suspect, increasingly popular development in work on utilitarianism.) On this alternative, then, the principle of utility is framed in terms of the maximization of the satisfaction of interests, where 'interests' is simply a term by which to refer to a variety of desires.

In addition to an explanation of utility, however, there is another integral part to the principle of utility; this is its scope. It must be made clear that it is the act's consequences as affecting everyone and not just the agent himself which are to be considered. For, at least as both are usually construed, the only major difference between ethical egoism and actutilitarianism is that the egoist is concerned with maximizing utility in his own case, so that only consequences which affect him bear upon the rightness and wrongness of his acts. In an act-utilitarianism, on the other hand, everyone affected by the act is to be considered, and to be considered equally, at least on the usual assumption of each to count for one and none for more than one. But if everyone affected by the act is to be considered, are we to consider the animals affected by our acts? As we saw earlier, virtually all utilitarians, present-day as well as classical, have wanted the scope of the principle of utility extended to animals, or, in any event, to the 'higher' animals. In this way, we obtain a characterization of the principle something like 'Always maximize net satisfaction of interests of animals as well as humans'; and this expanded characterization both accurately reflects present-day views on the interpretation of utility and on the scope of the principle of utility and is, in its present essentials, a plausible candidate for the principle of utility.

One implication of past chapters should now be apparent: concerned with the satisfaction of interests, the principle of utility can be extended to cover animals only if animals have interests; but animals have interests only if they have desires,[16] and these, I have argued, they do not have. Therefore,

[16] To allow that they have interests because they have needs leads, as I have shown earlier (Ch. VII), to counterintuitive results.

the principle of utility cannot be extended to cover them. But this is not the only or the only important problem here which the utilitarian must confront, and one of these problems is extremely serious indeed.

If I am to maximize the satisfaction of desires, which are the desires I am to concern myself with? To reply in terms of the maximization of present and/or future desires leads to problems.[17] To begin with, some of the things we desired yesterday we no longer desire today. It is difficult to know how to proceed with the principle of utility in the face of this fact, knowing as I do that, though I now desire revenge on my next-door neighbour for his carelessness with my lawn-mower, the likelihood is that I will have forgotten all about this episode in a few days. Secondly, what we desire at one time we sometimes not only do not desire later but also regard our earlier desiring of it as regrettable and wish that our desire then had not been satisfied. A person cured of alcoholism no longer desires what he earlier desired, and if the cure has been a complete success he almost certainly regards the satisfaction of his earlier desires as having been highly injurious to his health and so regrets the fact of their having been persistently satisfied. Thirdly, are the alcoholic's present desires, then, not to be maximized? But if it is the alcoholic's future desires which are to be maximized, we do not at the moment know (i) what these are or (ii) that he will seek treatment or (iii) whether the treatment will be successful. So if we try to decide on the basis of the principle of utility what to do in the alcoholic's case, we have nothing concrete whatever in terms of his future desires to put against his present, intense desire for drink. Yet, if we maximize the satisfaction of his present desires, we condemn him to a life of increasing alcoholism, with all the horrible consequences which typically ensue. Fourthly, changes in our desires also reflect changes in our circumstances and/or emotional states. My desires after having been insulted are different from what

---

[17] Many of these problems have been raised and discussed at length in a series of seminars held in Oxford each Trinity Term for some years running by James Griffin and Jonathan Glover (and, earlier, Derek Parfit). My discussion of these problems here, though not the anti-utilitarian point I use them to make, is indebted to these seminars and especially to several of Griffin's formal contributions.

they were before the insult; and it makes a good deal of difference whether the principle of utility is concerned with the satisfaction of my desires before the insult, and the onset of anger and outrage, or afterwards. Such emotional changes need not be so instantaneous, however, to produce the same problem. For a long time now, Bill's work has gone unnoticed by those who count and has had scorn heaped upon it by those who do not; his depression has grown increasingly intense, until, today, he has finally decided to put an end to his wretched existence. He now desires above all else to end his life. Tomorrow? He does not know what tomorrow will bring. Perhaps some important critic will have a good word for him, perhaps not; in any event, there is nothing to set against his present desire, which has been a long time growing, to end it all. To have maximized the satisfaction of his present desires some months ago would have yielded a result a good deal different from what will ensue now if his present desires are satisfied. Or does Bill refrain from applying the principle of utility until his depression lifts, whenever that is? Fifthly, conflict situations pose difficulties. Today, Bill desires to end it all; yesterday, however, he desired to carry on living, in order to see to his daughter's education. There is a conflict between desires in this case: yesterday, Bill's present desire was to live, today, it is to die; yesterday, his future desire was to die, and it conflicted with his then present desire, which was to live; and tomorrow, though he does not know what it will bring, it is possible that his then present desire will conflict with his desire at present to die. And if, yesterday, he was under an injunction to maximize the satisfaction of his *total* set of desires, present as well as future; and if, for the sake of argument, we concede him knowledge of what his future desires would be; then that total set of desires would have included a desire to live and a desire to die, and it is not clear how a principle of utility can accommodate itself to such a situation.

In view of these problems, it is not surprising that utilitarians have switched from present and/or future desires to rational ones, so that the principle of utility becomes concerned with the maximization of the satisfaction of rational desires. Rational desires are those desires we would have if we were not at present angry or under stress or under the influence of drink or suffering from depression and if we were rational, if we possessed knowledge of ourselves and of what we are and will be like, if we were well-informed about the world, about the situations we are likely to find ourselves in, and about the hopes, wishes, and expectations of other people, and if we possessed sufficient detachment to assess such knowledge and information calmly and carefully. Addiction to drink is not something I would desire if I were fully rational, knowledgeable, and well-informed about its progressively debilitating effects and if I were sufficiently detached to consider carefully this knowledge and information and the ghastly consequences which the persistent satisfaction of a desire for drink produces. Of course, it may turn out, as Griffin has urged, that many of our actual desires are rational ones, but there is certainly no necessity about this, as can be seen by thinking through my earlier examples.

The difficulty the utilitarian faces *vis-à-vis* animals is obvious: the principle of utility can only be extended to cover animals if animals have rational desires, and it is at the very least highly doubtful that they do. I shall not labour the point; but to ask what my dog would desire if it were fully rational, if it had knowledge of itself and of what it is and will be like, if it were well-informed about the world, about the hopes and wishes (of dogs and) of people, and about the situations it found and was likely to find itself in, and if it possessed sufficient detachment to assess such knowledge and information calmly and carefully is to ask a question which has no ready answer, except, perhaps, the steady insistence that, in the sense in which they are meant, my dog is none of these things. When I throw the stick, my dog fetches it; but whether it would do this if it were rational, knowledgeable about its future, and the rest of it, I have not the faintest idea. However, since I have grounds for thinking my dog is none of these things, yet since it always fetches the stick, what is in fact obtained by raising the question of what it would do or prefer to do *if it were* all these things?

There is a further difficulty here which ought not to be ignored. We can, at least very roughly, rank our rational desires in some form of hierarchy and can as a result achieve trade-offs between lower- and higher-level desires. For example, to take an extremely simple case, suppose I desire both a new boat and a new flat: I can buy the boat or take out a mortgage on the flat but not both. What do I do? I ask myself which of the two I desire more and rank the desires accordingly. But in deciding which of these two things I desire more, a host of factors enter. The boat, if bought, will depreciate, whereas the flat will appreciate; but the boat will be mine now, whereas the flat will not really be mine for many years. I can have the boat in the short term, but is not the flat in the long term more than adequate compensation? Then there is the horse I have desired for so long. And so it goes. I try to put my desires for these things into some sort of order, so that the dispersal of my funds coincides with the satisfaction of my higher-level desires or coincides with the satisfaction of so many of my lower-level desires that I am prepared to sacrifice the satisfaction of some of my higher-level ones.[18] As Griffin has remarked, rational desire orderings of this sort seem absolutely vital to our ordinary lives, given the overwhelming likelihood that only a very few of our desires can be satisfied at any one time. In turn, therefore, it seems absolutely vital that a utilitarianism be able to show how such a ranking is possible, especially if it is to have any chance whatever at solving the old conundrum of interpersonal comparisons of utility, which in the present discussion means interpersonal comparisons of strength of desire.[19]

Now in the case of my dog, can anything like a ranking of rational desires be achieved? Even if those who think he has desires simply agree to regard all his actual desires as rational ones, it is not obvious how one can do anything other than appeal to his instincts and their effect on him in the heat of the moment. When I put food before him, my dog eats it; when I throw the stick, he fetches it. Both he does unfailingly, unless he is distracted by some stronger impulse,

[18] An excellent and probing discussion of many of these issues is to be found in James Griffin's 'Are There Incommensurable Values?', *Philosophy and Public Affairs*, 7 (1977), 39-59.

[19] I leave aside here the interesting question of how *interspecies* comparisons of utility are to be carried out, except to observe that the problems surrounding them are likely to prove even more intractable than those surrounding interpersonal comparisons, on the solutions to which we have made only little progress.

such as, on occasion, sex; and in response to the question whether my dog desires or prefers eating to chasing sticks, I can only say he does both when the situations are to hand and no other impulse interferes. Several times, I have tried putting food before him and throwing a stick at the same time; each time he has sought neither the food nor the stick but stood looking at me. On the other hand, if I have not fed him all day, and I put food before him, absolutely nothing distracts him from eating, not even another dog. But then he is hungry and needs food; and it would be false to characterize the situation as his preferring food to the passing company of another dog.

Of course, this whole discussion presupposes that, given my dog has desires, all his actual desires are rational ones. This in itself is doubtful; after all, not even all of a human' being's desires are necessarily rational ones, as we have seen. In any event, I do not think a utilitarian will accept this trick of simply turning my dog's actual desires into rational ones; for I do not think he *can* accept it, without draining the phrase 'rational desire' of any and all significance. Such a loss of significance is completely unacceptable, obviously, since it is by means of rational desires that he hopes to meet our earlier difficulties surrounding present and/or future desires and the principle of utility. But if he does not turn all its actual desires into rational ones, how is he to tell which are my dog's rational desires? And if he cannot determine this, how is he to extend the principle of utility to cover my dog?

In sum, if the principle of utility is taken to be concerned with the satisfaction of *desires*, then it is arguable, because it is arguable that animals do not have desires, that the principle does not extend to them; and if the principle of utility is further taken to be concerned with the maximization of the satisfaction of *rational desires*, then it is further arguable, because it is arguable that animals do not have rational desires, that the principle does not extend to them. In this way, it certainly appears that, in the absence of some remedy, either the interpretation of utility in terms of the satisfaction of interests must be given up in favour of an interpretation which allows animals to have the principle of utility extended to them, or the scope of the principle must be restricted to the class of human beings, neither of which is an attractive option to many contemporary utilitarians.

XI

Pain, Interests, and Vegetarianism

The upshot of preceding chapters and the exploration of the psychological endowment animals would have to possess in order to have interests is apparent: animals either have interests in a sense which yields the counterintuitive result that things and man-made/manufactured objects have interests, and so, on the interest requirement, have or are candidates for having moral rights, or, if animals do not have beliefs or desires or rational desires or emotions or a moral psychology, and if they do not grasp propositions or make judgements or act for reasons, they do not have interests at all, and so, on the interest requirement, do not have and are not candidates for having moral rights. Accordingly, the Nelsonian argument for the moral rights of animals fails: its major premiss — that all and only beings which (can) have interests (can) have moral rights — is dubious, and its minor premiss — that animals as well as humans (can) have interests — is false.

So far as the minor premiss of Nelson's argument is concerned, there remains one final defence to consider. This consists in the claim that, even if all my earlier arguments succeed, it remains true that animals or at least some animals can feel pain, and *feeling pain is either a necessary or a sufficient condition for possessing interests*. In this chapter, I shall examine these possibilities in turn, beginning with the claim that being able to feel pain is a necessary condition for the possession of interests. For this is the stronger, more forceful of the two alternatives, and the one which, when one first considers the matter, particularly if one has read or been to any degree influenced by the classical utilitarians, is likely to be embraced. Certainly, it is the position most often adopted by others when I have discussed the matter with them.

I shall examine these two possibilities in a wider context. For it so happens that one of the best-known contemporary arguments in favour of vegetarianism turns fundamentally upon a view of pain as a necessary condition for the possession of interests.

PAIN AS A NECESSARY CONDITION

An enormous volume of material has already appeared on the conditions under which animals live and die on factory farms,[1] and more is almost certainly on the way. Much of this material is upsetting in the extreme, and it is difficult to imagine any normal person reading or hearing of it without being revolted. Indeed, our feeling of revulsion may be so intense that we simply can no longer bring ourselves to eat meat. In other words, we become vegetarians, not through any decision of principle, but through being unable to bring ourselves to continue to dine upon the flesh of animals. We become vegetarians in this way, however, only if we are revolted to a degree sufficient to overcome our fondness or liking for meat; and whether we are *going to be* sufficiently revolted by what we read and hear cannot be known in advance by the advocate of vegetarianism. If our liking for meat is in fact more intense than our revulsion at the suffering endured on factory farms, then we are going to remain meat-eaters, with the result that, if the vegetarian has grounded his case in an appeal to our feelings, then that case is in jeopardy. In order to protect himself, therefore, he is not likely to rest his case upon (an appeal to) the state and intensities of our feelings.

---

[1] For the uninitiated, a good introduction to this material is to be found in Singer's *Animal Liberation,* pp. 96–166. The notes to these pages, pp. 167–70, give the many sources of his material. Another well-known work in this regard is Ruth Harrison's *Animal Machines* (Vincent Stuart, London, 1964). A good, representative sample of the kinds of scientific experiments presently being conducted on animals can be found in Richard Ryder's *Victims of Science* (Davis-Poynter, London, 1975), in Dallas Pratt's *Painful Experiments on Animals* (Argus Archives, New York, 1977), and in *Alternatives to Laboratory Animals,* a journal of abstracts published in London by the Fund for the Replacement of Animals in Medical Experiments (FRAME).

What the vegetarian wants, surely, is that we should stop eating meat even if our liking for it *exceeds* our revulsion at the suffering endured on factory farms. And this would seem to be possible only if vegetarianism is based upon principle and not upon feeling. That is, if what the vegetarian wants is that we should stop eating meat even if we like eating it and even if our liking for it greatly exceeds our revulsion at the suffering of animals in being raised and slaughtered for food, then a decision to stop eating meat would seem to amount to a decision of principle. It does not *follow* that this principle, which becomes the ground or basis of our vegetarianism, will be a *moral* one; but the overwhelming likelihood is that it will be, in view of the fact that it must convince and compel us to give up eating meat even when our inclinations, habits, and feelings run strongly in the opposite direction. If vegetarianism *has* a moral basis, a ground rooted in moral principle, then all of us, if we take morality seriously, must earnestly examine our present eating practices, however intense our liking for meat.

In his book *Animal Liberation*, Peter Singer argues that vegetarianism has just such a basis in moral principle; and the whole point to his book is that, if we care about morality at all, this principle compels us to become vegetarians. In what follows, I deny that vegetarainism has the moral basis Singer alleges it has, and I deny this in a way which does not raise quibbles about whether I am taking morality seriously.

According to Singer, the principle of the equal consideration of interests 'requires us to be vegetarians' (p. 257). This is a moral principle (pp. 5–8), and states that 'the interests of every being affected by an action are to be taken into account and given the same weight as the like interests of any other being' (p. 6). Interests arise, Singer contends, from the capacity to feel pain, which he labels a 'prerequisite' for having interests at all (pp. 9, 185); and animals can and do suffer, can and do feel pain (pp. 10–19). The principle of the equal consideration of interests, therefore, applies to them, which in turn means that we are not morally justified in ignoring, disregarding, or otherwise neglecting their interests (pp. 9, 185). This, however, is precisely what factory farming does (pp. 9–10, 96–166). Factory farming is nothing more than modern methods of technology applied to the mass production of food for human consumption (p. 172); but this particular production line involves widespread and often intense suffering (pp. 100–66) and therein the systematic disregard and/or undervaluation of the interests of animals (pp. 9, 10), a disregard and/or undervaluation the moral seriousness of which is, if anything, *compounded* by the fact that alternative and health-sustaining sources of food are for the most part readily available to us (pp. 178–99). By forgoing meat in our diets, we can reduce, if not eliminate, this massive suffering of animals, merely through bringing market forces to bear upon factory farming (pp. 174–8). The smaller the demand for meat, the lower its price; the lower the price, the lower the profit; and the lower the profit, the fewer the animals that will be raised and slaughtered on factory farms. A serious concern for the suffering and interests of animals, then, as expressed through vegetarianism, which, after all, is effectively nothing more than the boycott of meat (p. 175), directly affects factory farming, the immediate source of so much of this suffering. Doubtless it may and will be suggested that someone opposed to inflicting suffering on animals but not to painlessly killing them could still consistently eat the flesh of animals that had been reared and slaughtered painlessly; but Singer rejects such a suggestion on three counts. First, it amounts to looking upon animals as in effect means to the end of satisfying our tastes for certain types of flesh, and factory farming is nothing more than the application of technological methods to this idea (p. 172); second, it is impossible to rear animals on a massive scale for human consumption without inflicting suffering (pp. 172–3); and third, even traditional methods of farming involve extensive suffering (p. 172). There is for Singer, then, no escaping the conclusion: if we take morality seriously, a genuine concern for the interests of animals and for the diminution of their suffering requires that we cease rearing and slaughtering animals for food and cease dining upon them (pp. 24, 257, 270–1).[2]

---

[2] Having now completed my exposition of Singer, I should perhaps stress what I hope in any event is apparent, viz. that his argument for vegetarianism does not rely upon or require the claim that animals possess moral rights. I am examining

Now there are a number of different strands to this argument;[3] but by far the most important is that which links the principle of the equal consideration of interests to animals. For without such a link, Singer cannot use this principle as the moral basis of his vegetarianism, and this, after all, is the point of his book (pp. 24, 257). As we have seen, this link is provided by the claim that animals have interests, since, obviously, only if animals *have* interests can the moral principle of the equal consideration of interests apply to them and require us to take their interests into account and accord them equal weight with the like interests of human beings. Thus, only if the claim that animals have interests is established can vegetarianism have the moral basis Singer alleges it has. In other words, I can deprive Singer of his moral basis to vegetarianism by severing the link between the principle of the equal consideration of interests and animals, and I can sever this link by showing, quite apart from my own, earlier arguments, that he has not established that animals do have interests.

Animals have interests, according to Singer, in virtue of the fact that they can suffer; and he emphasizes a number of times that the capacity for suffering is a 'prerequisite' for having interests at all (pp. 8, 9, 17, 185, 254). By 'prerequisite', I understand 'something required', in this case that the condition of being able to suffer be satisfied, if a creature is to have interests. That is, a prerequisite is *at least a necessary* condition, whereby I mean to allow that satisfaction of the condition may also suffice to establish the point at issue. In the United States, Philosophy 101 is a prerequisite for admission into Philosophy 201, in the sense that the successful completion of course 101 is at least a necessary

his argument here simply because it *does rely* upon the claim that pain is at least a necessary condition for the possession of interests. For a helpful discussion of many of the other arguments for vegetarianism, including those which do not rely upon the claims that animals possess interests and/or moral rights, see Michael Martin, 'A Critique of Moral Vegetarianism', *Reason Papers No. 3* (Fall 1976), 13–43.

[3] One of the more interesting strands is this: what sort of mistake would I be making if, though I gave the alleged interests of animals some weight, I did not give them the same weight as the like interests of human beings? After all, sometimes we accord the interests of children less and sometimes more weight than the like interests of adults.

condition for admission into course 201, while, in Britain, successful completion of Part I of the BA degree is a prerequisite or at least a necessary condition for admission into Part II of the degree. Singer is claiming, then, I take it, that the capacity for suffering is a necessary condition for the possession of interests, which condition, if satisfied, may also suffice for the possession of interests.

One can, of course, always try to prevent Singer from reaching this point in his argument by going back several stages and denying that animals can feel pain, so that, even if the capacity for suffering *is* a necessary (and perhaps sufficient) condition for possessing interests, animals cannot satisfy that condition. But the view that animals cannot feel pain, Singer contends, is obviously extreme (p. 10) and virtually indefensible, in view of modern studies on the behaviour of animals, on their nervous systems, and on their differing levels of sentiency (pp. 10–16, 184–92).

The above, in fact, is the only opponent which Singer discusses or envisages, so far as his claim about pain and animal interests is concerned; but there is, however, at least one other challenger in the field. This is the individual who argues, not that animals cannot feel pain, but rather that being able to feel pain is not a necessary condition or prerequisite for the possession of interests.

(One might fall back here and allege that pain is merely a sufficient condition for the possession of interests, and I will shortly have something to say about this ploy. But this is not Singer's tack. Singer is a utilitarian, cites Bentham on suffering and pain with approval (e.g. pp. 8–9), and finds it most amenable to his utilitarianism to regard pains and pleasures as the items upon which the moral principle of the equal consideration of interests is grounded. His whole approach and tone is one of suffering or pain as a necessary condition for the possession of interests:

The capacity for suffering and enjoyment is a *prerequisite* for *having interests at all*, a condition that must be satisfied before we can speak of interests in a meaningful way. It would be nonsense to say that it was not in the interests of a stone to be kicked along the road by a schoolboy. A stone does not have interests because it cannot suffer. (p. 9; author's italics.)

To have interests, in a strict nonmetaphorical sense, a being must be capable of suffering or experiencing pleasure. . . . If a being is not capable of suffering, or of enjoyment, there is nothing to take into account. (p. 185)

If Singer is not presenting a necessary condition here, if he does not mean at least a 'necessary condition' by 'prerequisite', then his book is seriously misleading at its very centre.)

Curiously enough, in view of its central importance, this prerequisite of Singer's for having interests is initially simply stated (pp. 8–9) and thereafter merely assumed (e.g. p. 185); and the fact that Singer *presumes* its truth and does not argue in its support shows, no doubt, that he has not *established* it. Nevertheless, it could still be true; so I myself am in need of an argument if I am going to cast doubt upon its truth. My argument is simply this: Singer's prerequisite for having interests is dubious, if not false, since we can and do speak of interests in cases where the capacity for feeling pain is muted in non-trivial ways and where this capacity is entirely absent.[4]

While serving in Vietnam, a soldier friend of mine received such severe and extensive head, spinal, and nervous injuries that, amongst other things, though he was conscious, he was no longer able to feel pain. Did he, therefore, cease to have interests? On Singer's prerequisite, it would seem that he did; but surely his interest in being cared for while ill was *more*, not less, pronounced because of his wounds? And what about his interest in having his wife and children looked after, and his interest in retaining his good name? Certainly, it would be very peculiar to maintain that one has an interest in a good name, only so long as one can feel pain; for one's good name can be sullied and one's interests thereby damaged whether or not one feels any pain in the process and, indeed, even if one remains forever in the dark about the allegations which do the harm. Certainly, too, this is an interest of my friend and others which the courts acknowledge and protect, even if the individual whose interests are in question cannot

---

[4] I do not make only a verbal point here, about what we can and do say. As will be seen, the cases which follow can be and are hotly contested, in ways which they could not be if Singer's prerequisite were correct.

feel pain. Of course, an action brought in a case such as my
friend's is brought by someone else on his behalf; but it does
not follow that it is not *his interests* which are in jeopardy of
being harmed and which the courts will and do protect.[5]

Another type of case which is relevant to the evaluation of
Singer's prerequisite is that exemplified by Karen Quinlan,[6]
in which an individual does not and cannot feel pain as the
result of being in a comatose state, which state can last from
a few hours to decades. Does Karen Quinlan have interests?
Once again, since she cannot feel pain, on Singer's prerequisite it appears that she does not; but here, too, I would

[5] I am trying to show that interests are conceded in such cases as this one by
appealing, first, to the way in which the cases are contested precisely because interests are attributed in them and, second, to the fact that the courts acknowledge
and protect the interests at risk in them. I came to the first part of this argument
by reflecting on cases such as my friend's and reaching the position (i) that the
individuals in such cases have vital concerns in respect of what happens to them
and theirs, (ii) that these vital concerns represent interests they have, (iii) that
these concerns are things in which they have an interest in spite of the fact that
they are things in which they cannot take an interest, and (iv) that these interests
do not simply vanish the moment an individual such as my friend steps upon an
anti-personnel mine or lapses into a coma. Having this part of the argument in mind,
which I will shortly develop further, I then saw how to wed it to the second part and
to anchor my criticism of Singer's prerequisite in the whole, as the result of reading
and reflecting upon the following passage in Joel Feinberg's *Social Philosophy*
(Prentice-Hall, Englewood Cliffs, N.J., 1973, p. 26): 'Legal writers classify interests in various ways. One of the more common lists "Interests of Personality,"
"Interests of Property," "Interests in Reputation," "Interest in Domestic Relations," and "Interest in Privacy," among others. A humanly inflicted harm is con-
ceived as the violation of one of a person's interests, an injury to something in
which he has a genuine stake. In the lawyer's usage, an interest is something a
person always possesses in some condition, something that can grow and flourish
or diminish and decay, but which can rarely be totally lost.' In my view, this is
not mere 'lawyer's usage'; on the contrary, it is an important fact in our thinking
about people that the stake they have in the concerns of life is not lost through,
for instance, having suffered damage to their nervous system. (The first part of
this chapter, then, owes a debt to pp. 26–7 of Feinberg's book, not least because
I am going to exploit the notion of having a stake in, in order to underpin the
first part of my argument here.)

[6] The case of Karen Ann Quinlan has become familiar, as the result of the
publicity surrounding her parents' petition to allow her to die and her doctors'
refusal to go along with this. (Both parties, of course, clearly believed that she was
not already dead; see Ch. III, n. 11). Among the books on the case, see M.D.
Heifetz *et al.*, *The Right to Die* (Berkley Publishing Corporation, New York,
1975); and B.D. Colen, *Karen Ann Quinlan: Dying in the Age of Eternal Life*
(Nash Publishing Co., New York, 1976). Of related interest is *Ethical Issues in
Death and Dying*, eds. T.L. Beauchamp, S. Perlin (Prentice-Hall, Englewood
Cliffs, N.J., 1978), Part IV.

urge on her behalf those considerations presented on behalf of my friend. And other considerations spring to mind at once. For example, if a photographer slips into her room and photographs Karen Quinlan, her interest in having her privacy respected is presumably not violated, since she has no interests. Importantly, the argument that her privacy cannot be invaded because she cannot *know* her privacy is invaded — a highly questionable argument, in any event — is not Singer's; for according to his prerequisite, it is not because a Karen Quinlan cannot *know* anything but because she cannot *feel pain* that she has no interests. In other words, the state of her knowledge is immaterial to the question of whether she has interests, a view which an animal liberationist such as Singer seems bound to be attracted by, since people in general are much more ready to accept that animals feel pain than they are to accept that they can have knowledge. Thus, for Singer, because she can feel no pain, Karen Quinlan can have no interests, not even an interest in having her privacy respected, which, even in non-comatose individuals like ourselves, seems to be an interest that has nothing whatever to do with being able to feel pain. Again, if we are trying to discover whether it would be right to switch off Karen Quinlan's life-sustaining machines, we can consult the interests of her parents, her doctors, the hospital staff, the taxpayers, and so on; but if Singer is right, we cannot include among the interests to be consulted her own, since she does not have any. Hence the individual who, in an ordinary, straightforward sense of the term, may well die if the life-sustaining machines are switched off is deemed to have no interest whatever to be weighed in deciding whether to switch them off, and not because she cannot know of, consent to, or appreciate this decision, but merely because she cannot feel pain.[7] The point has moral implications: her

---

[7] On the question of whether the comatose are already dead, see Ch. III, n.11. In the Quinlan case, the New Jersey Superior Court decided in 1976 that the respirator could be switched off, and this was subsequently done, without, much to the surprise of the doctors, death ensuing. This fact does not affect my point here, which is that, on Singer's prerequisite, Karen Quinlan has no interests to be weighed in reaching the decision to turn off the respirator, though it is she who is affected by that decision. (For a discussion of whether turning off the respirator amounts to injuring Karen Quinlan, see Marvin Kohl, 'Euthanasia and the Right

doctors and others have argued that Karen Quinlan's interests will best be served if her life-sustaining machines are left on, whereas her parents and others have argued that her interests will best be served if she is allowed 'to die with dignity'. On Singer's prerequisite, however, both doctors and parents are wrong in thinking Karen Quinlan has any interests at all, so the questions of how to weigh her interests morally, of how much weight to give them, and of how best to serve them cannot even arise in the first place. It is impossible, therefore, to ignore, undervalue, or damage Karen Quinlan's interests, which leaves us with the bizarre conclusion that any decision about the machines, any decision whatever, including the decision to turn off the machines for the fun of it, cannot fail to do justice to her interests.

Now one of the things which underlies our talk of interests in cases like these is this: we regard my friend and Karen Quinlan as human beings or persons, and, in virtue of that fact, deem them to have a genuine stake in certain things, quite independently of whether they can feel pain; and what we deem them to have a genuine stake in, we deem them to have an interest in.[8] In this way, human beings or persons are deemed to have a genuine stake and, therefore, an interest in

to Life', in *Philosophical Medical Ethics: Its Nature and Significance,* ed. S.F. Spicker, H.T. Engelhardt, Jr. (D. Reidel, Dordrecht, 1977), pp. 79 ff. Of related interest are H.K. Beecher's 'Ethical Problems Created by the Hopelessly Unconscious Patient', *New England Journal of Medicine,* 278 (1968), 1425–30; and G. Fletcher's 'Prolonging Life', 42 *Washington Law Review* [1967] 999.) The complete record of the Quinlan case in the New Jersey Superior Court, Morristown, New Jersey, including medical testimony, can be found in *In the Matter of Karen Quinlan* (University Publications of America, Inc., Arlington, Virginia, 1975, 1976).

Singer has indicated to me that, though the implications I spell out here will appear to many as unfortunate ones, just as the labelling of such people as 'vegetables' is to me regrettable, he still prefers the view that Karen Quinlan has no interests. If I read Feinberg correctly, he is of the same opinion; see 'The Rights of Animals and Unborn Generations', pp. 60 f.

[8] See n. 5 above; see also Feinberg, *Social Philosophy*, p. 26. This sense of 'interest' is probably the most common in ordinary parlance; after all, a person who has an interest in something often has a stake, a financial stake at that, in that thing. But it would be wrong to treat the financial overtones of this sense as basic to it; for a husband and father has a stake in the vital concerns of life, both for himself and his family, and it would be wholly erroneous to think that the stake he has in what happens to his wife and children is tied to his financial support of them. Rather, as I shall argue, they are a part of his extended well-being, in respect of which human beings typically have certain desires.

receiving medical attention while ill, in having their families cared for, in retaining their good name, in having their privacy respected, and in life itself. Whether they are able to feel pain is neither here nor there to their being deemed to have these interests, and the law reflects this fact. For one can invade the privacy of or libel, for example, comatose as well as non-comatose individuals; and it is *neither a legal nor a moral* defence to libel that the individual libelled cannot feel pain. Thus, the interests of human beings or persons can be harmed, even though, as in the cases of my friend and Karen Quinlan, those whose interests they are cannot thereby be physically hurt; and this fact too the law recognizes, in distinguishing between harming interests and hurting individuals and in allowing the interests of individuals to be harmed even though these same individuals are not thereby hurt, as when my privacy is invaded unknown to me.[9]

If, then, one is going to call into question whether my friend and Karen Quinlan have interests, it would seem that one must show not that they cannot feel pain but that — what is by no means the same thing — they are not human beings or persons. This is brought out very clearly, I think, in the controversy surrounding another type of case which deserves mention in respect of evaluating Singer's prerequisite, namely that of abortion. For many have wanted to argue that, in addition to the interests of the mother, the father, the other members of the family, society, etc., there are the interests of the foetus to consider, both in deciding in individual cases whether to abort and in deciding on the moral rightness of abortion *per se*. Yet, though the foetus may react to stimuli, there is no ready consensus that it feels pain. Those who argue that the foetus *does have interests* typically advance as the ground for their view that the foetus is a human being or person; but there is no attempt whatever on their part to identify being a human being or person with being able to feel pain, since we do not allow that everything which might be able to feel pain is a human being or person, and animals are precisely the exception we have in mind. Of

[9] See Feinberg, *Social Philosophy*, p. 27; see also his 'The Rights of Animals and Unborn Generations', pp. 59 f.

course, accepting this point, one may nevertheless go on to insist that, because it remains unborn, the foetus *is not* a human being or person and, therefore, has no interests;[10] and this challenge — that the foetus is not a human being or person — highlights the claim I think we shall want established, both in this case and in those of my friend and Karen Quinlan, if we are to take the ascription of interests in these cases to be misplaced. It is precisely because some people *are* doubtful that the foetus is a human being or person, a doubt which is far less likely to arise or to be widespread in the cases of my friend and Karen Quinlan, that talk of weighing the interests of the foetus is sometimes objected to.

Once the decision to consider foetuses human beings or persons has been taken, however, it seems clear that we then (i) deem foetuses to have interests, (ii) extend moral and perhaps legal protection to these interests, and (iii) commit ourselves to weighing those interests in reaching decisions affecting foetuses. In the cases of my friend and Karen Quinlan, on the other hand, a decision of this sort is unnecessary, since they have been and are human beings or persons and so are already deemed to have interests, which can be legally and morally protected and which can be considered and weighed in reaching decisions affecting them. Of course in the last of these two cases it is sometimes doubted that the being in question still is a human being or person, though almost always a distinction is drawn; that is, it is sometimes argued that a human 'vegetable', though a human being, has ceased to be a person.[11] In this regard, it is significant that human 'vegetables', even if we concede for the sake of argument that they are not persons but merely human beings, can, for example, be libelled and have their privacy invaded and can have their interests in these regards protected by the courts, as well as by the rest of us adopting moral sanctions against the offending parties.

---

[10] This is the typical utilitarian position (minus my comments about our deeming a creature to be a human being or person). Singer has indicated to me that he accepts it entirely and so regards foetuses as lacking all interests. Feinberg accepts it as well; see 'The Rights of Animals and Unborn Generations', pp. 62 f.

[11] Michael Tooley's paper 'Abortion and Infanticide' is sometimes cited in this connection. See Ch. VIII.

None of the above cases hold any comfort for Singer. This is not only because we do not regard being able to feel pain as having anything essentially to do with them, so far as the ascription of interests goes, and because we do not identify or otherwise equate being a human being or person with being able to feel pain, but also because Singer thinks animals have interests and so is most unlikely to accept being a human being or person as a prerequisite for having interests. I do not, however, wish to be misunderstood: I am not defending anything about these cases. I am not suggesting that we should continue to talk of interests in them, that we should not reform the law in order to avoid having to concede interests to my friend and Karen Quinlan, that we should not be at liberty to photograph and say what we like about them, that we should not be at liberty to switch off their life-sustaining machines, that we should not be able to regard and to dispose of foetuses in any way we like, and that we should not drop altogether the elusive talk of being a human being or person. Some of these things I think, others I do not. All I am maintaining is that, *contra* Singer, we can and do speak of the interests of my friend and Karen Quinlan, can and do acknowledge moral and legal protection of these interests, can and do concede that their interests are able to be harmed and benefited by us, can and do assign moral blame and legal responsibility in respect of such harm, in spite of the fact that these individuals are not able to feel pain. Unless, therefore, Singer turns his prerequisite for having interests into a stipulative one, so that it now becomes true by stipulation that only beings which are able to feel pain have interests, we have grounds for rejecting that prerequisite as false.

I suppose it is possible that the cases of my friend, Karen Quinlan, and, for that matter, the foetus may be regarded by some in this light: they are all cases where the capacity for feeling pain is simply muted, though in non-trivial ways. (By a 'trivial' muting of the capacity for feeling pain I have in mind not only treatment by anaesthetic and by acupuncture but also, and more seriously, cases of repetitive hysteria and of certain types of short-lived paralysis.) In other words, it might be argued that, though none of the three do feel pain, nevertheless, in virtue of the fact that they all possess a nervous system remarkably similar to our own, they in that sense *have the capacity* to feel pain.[12] I think this argument seriously misdescribes these cases: it is not merely that, for example, Karen Quinlan does not feel pain but also that she *cannot*; indeed, I think this is part of what we are describing when we describe someone as being 'in a coma'. But however this may be, there is a much stronger reply to the present argument, namely that we can and do speak of interests in cases where the capacity for feeling pain, construed *either* in its end-stage as, for example, actually having certain unpleasant sensations *or* as having a nervous system remarkably similar to our own, is entirely absent.

For example, much of the present writing and thinking on ecology and the environment is premissed on the fact that future beings, beings which do not now exist or feel pain or have the capacity to feel pain, nevertheless have interests. (On pp. 254–5, Singer himself appears to acknowledge this point, and he goes on to treat the case of future beings as a 'qualification' to his position. Importantly, I should stress that they only require to be noted as exceptions or qualifications if the capacity to feel pain is a necessary condition for the possession of interests. For if it were merely a sufficient condition, so that beings could straightforwardly lack it and still have interests, the case of future beings would not be an exception or qualification to Singer's position.) Thus, many people agree with Singer that we can harm the interests of future generations by wholesale pollution of the environment and by indiscriminately using up natural resources, whereas, by curbing our destructive tendencies in the name of progress and by conserving and even in some cases increasing our natural resources, they think we can protect, if not benefit, the interests of future generations.[13] But none of these future beings whose interests they think we can presently harm and benefit now feel pain or have the capacity to

[12] See Ch. III, n. 10. Something of the sort seems to be true as well for Mary Ann Warren; see 'Do Potential People Have Moral Rights?', p. 284.

[13] Singer, then, distinguishes the case of future people from the case of foetuses. Strange as it may seem to many, this is not at all uncommon today; see, for example, Feinberg, 'The Rights of Animals and Unborn Generations', pp. 64 ff.

feel pain; if, then, these beings have interests, as more and more people, including the courts, appear to believe, it cannot be in virtue of the structure of their nervous system. Here, also, we find that we can distinguish between hurting individuals and harming their interests; for though by destroying the quality of the environment we cannot hurt individuals who do not now exist, it is increasingly thought that we can harm their interests, which more and more people are convinced must be protected by legislation.

But such cases as these are not necessary to make the point; there are, after all, the more mundane cases, which by no means spring from our only recently revived concern with the environment. For instance, to give the best-known example, it has long been the policy in many Scandinavian communities to plant a tree for every tree cut. The interests of future generations are held to be straightforwardly affected by (and responsible for) this policy, which is vigorously policed, since nearly all of the trees planted will not reach their maturity and so be cut for decades, long after those who planted them have gone and new generations have appeared to cut and thereby to earn a living by means of them.

Since I have referred to the law several times already, let me give a legal example which illustrates my point here very clearly. We are all familiar with trust funds, in which a capital sum is left in trust *by* someone *to* someone else. Now it is perfectly possible and not at all unusual to find people leaving money to their grandchildren, who may as yet be unconceived. And if the trustee of this money misuses it, then the courts can be and are used to protect the interests of those who as yet do not exist, feel pain, or have the capacity to feel pain.[14] One's temptation, such as it is, to say that it is the grandparents' interests which are being protected, the courts notwithstanding, is avoided by supposing the trustee's misuse of funds and the subsequent lawsuit occur after the

---

[14] I owe this example to R.M. Hare. In discussing whether dead people can have rights, Feinberg uses the example of an insurance policy the benefits of which accrue to someone else after one's death ('The Rights of Animals and Unborn Generations', p. 57); adapting this example to my present purpose, nothing, so far as I know, prevents the drawing up of an insurance policy which benefits one's as yet unconceived grandchildren.

grandparents' deaths; and if one nevertheless wants simply to insist that it is the grandparents' interests which are being protected even after they are dead, then one seems committed to the view that dead people have interests.[15] In any event, nothing here is of use to Singer: if it is the grandchild's interests which are protected by the courts, as, indeed, they claim, then we have the counter-example as I have given it, whereas if one wants to go out on a limb and claim that, the courts notwithstanding, it is the grandparents' interests which are protected, then dead people have interests, even though they do not feel pain and lack the capacity to feel pain.

Here also, then, unless Singer turns his prerequisite for having interests into a stipulative one, so that it becomes true by stipulation that only beings which have the capacity to feel pain have interests, we have grounds for rejecting that prerequisite as false.

Finally, there is the naïve person and the issue of similarity to consider. Foetuses need nourishment, babies need nourishment, and the comatose need nourishment; and a naïve (and perhaps not-so-naïve) person would doubtless say that receiving nourishment regularly is in each of their interests. With regular nourishment, each persists; without regular nourishment, each ceases to persist. None of the three know, believe, or judge that receiving nourishment is necessary to their persistence; none of the three are conscious or aware of the fact that regular nourishment is necessary to the persistence of creatures of their kind; none of the three can in the usual sense provide themselves with the requisites necessary to their own persistence or arrange conditions such that these requisites will in the nature of things be secured them; and none of the three can undertake their own nourishment, at least in any sense of 'undertake' which is other than deviant and which implies agency. Plainly, too, none of the three have any idea either as to what nourishment is or as to what specific items in their respective cases will in fact provide the nourishment necessary to their persistence. If the naïve person consults a theologian, he is likely to be told that

[15] I have explored the issue of whether dead people have interests in my paper 'Do the Dead Have Interests?', which I am preparing for publication.

each of these creatures possesses an immortal soul; if he consults a lawyer, he is likely to be told that each of them can have interests before the law, which the courts can and do protect; and if he consults a doctor, he is likely to be told that regular nourishment and life support systems generally are necessary to the persistence of each, and, for that very reason, I suspect, to be told that regular nourishment and life support aids are in the interests of each. To a naïve person, in other words, these cases look remarkably alike; yet, rather puzzlingly, if Singer is right, receiving nourishment regularly can only be in the interests of the baby (only the baby feels pain), in spite of the fact that foetuses and the comatose, just as the baby, will cease to persist if denied regular nourishment. To say that these cases look remarkably alike to a naïve person is not to say that he thinks no distinctions can be drawn among them; of course, he thinks that some can. But it is to say that, when he encounters the claim that they are *radically different*, and when he finds that the radical difference consists in the fact that the baby can feel pain whereas the other two cannot, he will think he is entitled to ask, in virtue of the many similarities he finds among the cases, why it is being able to feel pain that is singled out in this way and given such extraordinary emphasis. If the reason is that Singer thinks that being able to feel pain is necessary in order to have interests, then Singer is wrong, as my earlier examples are intended to show; and if, as I suspect, the reason ultimately is that it is most amenable and conducive to Singer's utilitarianism to use pain to separate out the cases in this way, then the naïve person can hardly be condemned for failing to find this a particularly convincing reason for giving up his own emphasis upon the similarities amongst them.

On the strength of all the above sorts of cases, then, I conclude that Singer is mistaken in thinking that being able to feel pain is a prerequisite or at least a necessary condition for having interests. He has not, therefore, even begun to establish that animals actually have any interests, so that his link between the moral principle of the equal consideration of interests and animals is severed. With this link severed, it follows that vegetarianism does not have the moral basis

Singer alleges it has, a conclusion reached, plainly, without my having in the least to take morality less seriously than others do.

A final word on the examples of this section is required. If pain has nothing to do with them, what, then, does? The view which I think underlies them is this: my friend, Karen Quinlan, foetuses, and future beings either are or will be human beings; we deem human beings to have a stake in certain things; and what we deem them to have a stake in we deem them to have an interest in. Since we do not deem pigs and chickens to be human beings (or, for that matter, if one wants to distinguish, to be persons), we do not on this view concede them interests.

If we identify a creature as a human being, we deem it to have a stake in certain things. Which things? I think the answer is just those things which human beings typically desire (in respect of their general well-being), and we know what sorts of things *these* are by having been among and come to know something of human beings. Thus, we take my friend to be a human being and, invoking our knowledge of what human beings typically desire, deem him to have a stake in having his wife and children looked after. Typically, human beings desire privacy in respect of their personal lives, so unless one is prepared to exclude Karen Quinlan from the class of human beings we shall deem her to have a stake in such privacy. Foetuses and future beings will become human beings, so in trying to decide between two social policies, the full effects of which will not be produced until a good many years hence, we have reason to consider these future human beings and to make use of our knowledge of the desires typical of human beings, in deciding between these policies. The ascription of interests in these cases, then, is grounded upon our identifying the creatures in question as human beings; therefore, as I indicated earlier in this chapter, unless doubts can be raised about whether a particular creature *is* a human being — and remarks about pain are not going to do the trick, as even Singer himself concedes in respect of future human beings — we shall concede it a stake and so an interest in those things typically desired by human beings (in respect of their general well-being).

Thus, the sense of 'interest' bound up with desire, as in the sentence 'John has an interest in good health', arguably includes, albeit indirectly, those desires typical of John's kind (in respect of general well-being); and a desire for health and over-all well-being is just such a desire.[16] In this way, we can capture a further distinction,[17] between 'John has an interest in good health' and 'John takes an interest in good health'. A desire for good health is one important desire typical of human beings (in respect of their general well-being), so, even if comatose, John can and will be deemed to have a stake and so an interest in good health. He cannot, however, take an interest in good health. For in order to take an interest in good health, just as to take an interest in moral philosophy and animal rights, obviously, one must be giving time, effort, and consideration to it, must be from time to time applying oneself to secure it, as the result of which one inevitably comes to have further wishes and desires with respect to it; and the comatose cannot apply themselves to anything. Likewise, though we consider future human beings to have an interest in the quality of the environment, we do not consider them to take an interest in it; and though my friend has an interest in what happens to his wife and children, he cannot at present take an interest in what happens to them. It is on this view, then, a mistake always to conflate having an interest with taking an interest, a distinction which it seems especially important to observe in comatose cases; for though Karen Quinlan cannot take an interest in what happens to her, it does not follow — and I am inclined to think it dangerous to think otherwise — that she does not have an interest in what happens to her.

PAIN AS A SUFFICIENT CONDITION

It is possible, appearances notwithstanding, that Singer's case for vegetarianism will be taken to revolve around the claim

---

[16] This is not the point Feinberg is making (*Social Philosophy*, p. 26), when he tries to show that, though a man does not desire X, nevertheless X can integrate a man's total set of desires so as to give him a net balance of desire-fulfilment and so in this way still bear a connection with his desires.

[17] Alan White's discussion of this distinction is most fruitful; see above, Ch. X, n. 1.

that being able to feel pain is a sufficient condition for the possession of interests. In other words, by 'prerequisite', it is possible, in spite of the passages I have quoted to the contrary, that we are to understand a sufficient condition. A word on this possibility, therefore, is required.

The major difficulty with the claim that being able to feel pain is a sufficient condition for the possession of interests is that it is an unargued claim. Certainly Singer nowhere argues for it in *Animal Liberation*, nor do I know of an argument in the literature on animal rights and vegetarianism or on moral rights in general specifically devoted to establishing it. Of course, assuming the claim to be true and then taking its truth for granted has the convenient consequence of eliminating counter-examples in respect of animals; for to point to animals as creatures which feel pain but do not have interests only invites the retort that, if they feel pain, then that suffices to endow them with interests. In this way, the burden of proof is quietly shifted from the back of the proponent of the claim on to the back of the individual who queries whether animals do have interests.

Merely saying that X is a necessary or a sufficient or a necessary and sufficient condition for Y does not make it so. Argument is needed, and argument is precisely what is lacking. Singer's whole case for a moral basis to vegetarianism rests upon the claim that being able to feel pain is a 'prerequisite' for having interests; yet, to establish this crucial claim, he simply quotes favourably a passage from Bentham, which itself only states the claim, and passes on.[18] Nor is Singer alone in shunning argument: recent discussions of animal rights and of moral rights in general commonly betray this sort of thing. For example, in his book *Animal Rights*, Andrew Linzey suggests that, if we take sentiency (understood as being able to experience pain) as a 'criterion' for the possession of moral rights, then animals can have such rights;[19] but why should we take sentiency as a 'criterion' for the possession of rights in the first place? Linzey has no answer to this question, except to observe that, if we were to adopt such a 'criterion', we might obtain a view of the issues

[18] *Animal Liberation*, p. 9.
[19] *Animal Rights*, p. 26.

which is more favourable to animals than some other views.[20] Even if true, and even if we want a view of the issues which is favourable (or more favourable than some other view) to animals, this would not show that sentiency actually *is* a criterion for the possession of moral rights. Again, in her noteworthy paper 'Do Potential People Have Moral Rights?', Mary Ann Warren claims that 'sentience is a necessary and sufficient condition for the possession of moral rights'.[21] And what is her argument to support this claim? It is this:

. . . morality is or ought to be a system designed to promote the interests of sentient beings. Which sentient beings? Ideally, all there are and all there ever will be. Sentience is the ultimate source of all moral rights; a being that has experiences and that prefers experiences of some sorts to those of other sorts, has on that basis alone a prima facie right that those preferences be respected by beings that have the intelligence to comprehend this fact.[22]

Even if one happens to agree with all these assertions, as I know a good many people do, we have not really been given any reason to think that what Warren says is the case.

Perhaps understandably enough, what has gone wrong in these cases, I think, is that a value judgement about the intrinsic evilness of pain has come to take the place of argument. That is, a moral conviction that pain is an intrinsic evil is in fact the ultimate ground for the claim that being able to feel pain is a necessary or sufficient or necessary and sufficient condition for possessing interests and/or rights. In his widely influential paper 'The Moral Basis of Vegetarianism', Regan has this to say:

. . . if it is true that animals can and do experience pain; and if, furthermore, it is true, as I think it is, that pain is an intrinsic evil; then it must be true that the painful experience of an animal is, considered intrinsically, just as much of an evil as a comparable experience of a human being.[23]

And Regan's support for the claim that pain is an intrinsic evil? This claim, he says, is a 'value judgement'.[24] This represents at bottom, I believe, the central core of what is common not only to the work of Singer, Linzey, Warren, and Regan

---

[20] Ibid. 26 ff.   [21] p. 284.   [22] p. 283.
[23] pp. 186-7.   [24] p. 187.

himself but also to the work of all those who want to make sentiency out to be either the prerequisite for having interests or the prerequisite for having rights (or both).

This value judgement, however, compounds our problem. As we have seen, Singer's claim that being able to feel pain is a 'prerequisite' for having interests is unargued for; but it seems reasonable to suppose, given his fondness for Bentham, that the alleged intrinsic evilness of pain is intimately connected with this pre-eminent role pain is assigned in determining the possession of interests. If, however, we seek for the argument by which he shows that pain *is* an intrinsic evil, we shall seek in vain; there is not one to be found. Nor do Linzey, Warren, or Regan assist us in this regard either. In Chapter IV I mentioned some of the problems surrounding the very concept of intrinsic value, including the charge that it lacks a clear analysis, if it is not actually incoherent; and I shall not rehearse these complaints again. Instead, I want here to draw attention to one obvious aspect of our moral autonomy and its effect upon the issue of what possesses intrinsic value.

I am aware, as many vegetarians at a conference on animal rights at Trinity College, Cambridge in August 1977 were quick to point out to me, that one very prominent view of intrinsic value is that it is not something one argues for and establishes but something much more primitive than this; it is something which, so to speak, one finds or 'sees' in things. For example, some people claim that human life is intrinsically valuable. Generally speaking, what I think they mean when they say this is that they do not justify, for instance, acts of respecting human life in terms of some other value, such as the production of greater amounts of pleasure, but in terms of itself. If one cannot accept that human life is intrinsically valuable, if one cannot regard or 'see' human life in this way, then there is a clear sense in which one's justification of acts of respecting human life — if, indeed, one can justify them — is going to be at odds with the justification of one who does accept or 'see' this. The difference in justification reflects the difference in values.

Now the fact of the matter is, however, that we are autonomous agents so far as 'seeing' things as intrinsically valuable

PAIN, INTERESTS, AND VEGETARIANISM   161

is concerned, with the autonomy to find human life and
pain lacking in intrinsic value as well as otherwise. In other
words, it is not as if, for some reason of logic, we *have to
make* Regan's value judgement, so that Singer, for example,
might be thought in this way justified in simply making use
of such a judgement to ground his 'prerequisite' for interests.
Failure to face up to our autonomy in this regard results in a
failure to argue with those who do not find in pain an
intrinsic evil or with those who do not think anything in this
world possessed of intrinsic value or with those who do not
believe the notion of intrinsic value, value apart from the
specific aims and purposes of valuers, to be a coherent one.
One wants to say, 'Show me that pain is an intrinsic evil'; to
find the issue unargued, or to be told that it is not the sort of
thing which can be argued and shown, and then to see that
the value judgement that pain is an intrinsic evil plays a vital
role in the case for a moral basis to vegetarianism, is at the
very least bound to make the philosopher and anyone else in
search of arguments sceptical about the case erected upon
such a basis. (Though in different terms and for a different
purpose, my objection here about whether pain is an intrinsic
evil is also raised and discussed by Hare in his article 'Pain
and Evil', with which I am largely in agreement.)

Why *should* unpleasant sensations be regarded as intrinsically evil? The reply that a good many utilitarian theories
demand that they be cuts no ice whatever with someone who
is not a utilitarian. The point is worth pausing over. In
Roman Catholic and Anglican orthodoxy, for example,
though cardinal sins are regarded as intrinsically evil, the
mere having of unpleasant sensations is not. Sin and unpleasant sensations are not the same thing, as Peter Geach has
recently stressed in his discussion of animal pain in *Providence
and Evil*.[25] One can sin without inflicting unpleasant sensations, and one can inflict unpleasant sensations without
sinning. It is sin, not pain, which exercises the orthodox
Christian, sin and not pain which he is anxious to guard

[25] Cambridge University Press, Cambridge, 1977, pp. 67–83. Geach's main
point in these pages is that the pains of animals cannot morally be attributed to
God, since sympathy with these pains cannot be a virtue to a nature, the Divine
Nature, which is in no wise animal.

against. If the alternative to blaspheming is suffering un-
pleasantness, this is literally not a choice situation to the
orthodox; for sin is not to be committed merely in order to
avoid inflicting pain, either upon oneself or others. It is certainly not clear that the orthodox are *obviously* wrong in regarding sin but not pain as an intrinsic evil.

In short, we plumb the true depths of the reader's predica-
ment *vis-à-vis* Singer's book only when we realize that he
provides neither an argument to show that being able to feel
pain *is* a 'prerequisite' for having interests nor, if we assume
that his claim is supposed to be intimately connected with
and perhaps even to reflect the alleged intrinsic evilness of
pain, an argument to show that pain *is* intrinsically evil. Yet
his case for animal interests, and through interests a moral
basis to vegetarianism, turns upon the first of these, which
in turn connects with the second.

What we have so far, however, is a purely negative attack
upon Singer and the contention that his 'prerequisite', since
it cannot be a necessary condition for the possession of interests, must, therefore, be a sufficient condition.

A more positive line is possible. Either there is more than
one sufficient condition for the possession of interests or
there is only this one, viz., being able to feel pain. If there is
only this one, and it is, after all, all that Singer endorses or
thinks required to make his case, as we have seen; and if a
creature must be able to feel pain in order to have interests,
as Singer alleges; then it would appear that being able to feel
pain becomes a necessary and sufficient condition for the
possession of interests. But I have earlier in this chapter already shown that pain is not a necessary condition for having
interests. If, however, there is more than one sufficient condition for the possession of interests, then what are these
others? More especially, how are they related to the condition of being able to feel pain? On these questions, Singer
is silent; it is being able to feel pain alone which is, he says,
the 'prerequisite' for animal interests. (Nor is he alone in
this: as the literature attests, pain is by far the principal hope
of the animal rights/vegetarian camp.) The effect, I believe,
is to turn pain into a necessary and sufficient condition for
the possession of interests, and I can show this view mistaken

by showing that pain is not a necessary condition for having interests.

Let me develop this positive line a bit further. What underlay the earlier examples of this chapter was the view that my friend, Karen Quinlan, foetuses, and future beings either are or will be human beings and that they have a stake and, therefore, an interest in those things which creatures of their kind typically desire. Now one might try to gloss my discussion of these examples by suggesting that being human is a sufficient condition for possessing interests. If so, then what is the relationship between *this* sufficient condition and the sufficient condition of being able to feel pain? Plainly, no one such as Singer, who wants animals to have interests, can regard being human and being able to feel pain as *a set* of sufficient conditions, with the occurrence or presence of *the set* as what is required in order to establish the presence of interests; for this set excludes animals from the class of interest-holders.

No, it is not accidental that Singer appeals to pain and to nothing else whatever in order to make a case for animal interests, or that, for example, Linzey in *Animal Rights* appeals only to pain in order to make a case for animal rights; for anything else, if it is to form part of *a set* of sufficient conditions, runs the risk of jeopardizing the inclusion of animals within the class of interest-holders and/or right-holders. The reason for this is obvious from past chapters: to everyone except rabid Cartesians (who, I expect, are an extinct species anyway), animals feel pain, or, as I would prefer to say, since I think they lack this concept, have unpleasant sensations; on nothing else on which one is likely to base the possession of interests and/or rights is there anything like this degree of agreement over the case of animals. For example, I have already argued that animals do not have desires, beliefs, language, emotions, reasons, etc.; so to rely upon one of these, together with being able to feel pain, in order to form a set of sufficient conditions for interests and/or rights results in the exclusion of animals from the relevant class. The same is true for the other possible grounds we have touched upon; thus, if being able to feel pain and rationality are cited as the set of sufficient conditions for the possession of interests and/or rights, then there is going to be wide-spread disagreement on whether animals are rational and very widespread disagreement if one looks at all but a few (types of) animals or if one uses any but very minimal tests of rationality. No, appealing to pain and only to pain is important to Singer and the others here, since it is, today, non-controversial that animals have or can have unpleasant sensations; to base one's argument for animal interests and/or rights on anything else in addition to this places in jeopardy the reasonably secure ground of that argument.

The position, then, is this: being able to feel pain is, according to Singer, the one and only 'prerequisite' for the possession of interests, and beings which cannot feel pain cannot, he stresses, have interests. In this way, being able to feel pain is, I think, turned into a necessary and sufficient condition for having interests, and this view succumbs to the earlier argument of this chapter.

I should like to conclude this section on a slightly different though closely related note, which recalls one of the issues touched upon at the end of Chapter IV. As an alleged sufficient condition for interests and/or rights, pain is intended to ensure the *inclusion* of animals within the relevant class; as an alleged necessary condition for interests and/or rights, pain ensures the *exclusion* of rocks, trees, rivers, valleys, mountains, and the rest of non-sentient nature from the relevant class.

This view of pain (the only view actually in Singer's book, I maintain) as a necessary condition for the possession of interests (and in other writers, rights) has brought Singer (and the others) sharply into conflict with conservationists and environmental rightists. Some passages from John Rodman's excellent piece 'The Liberation of Nature?', which I made use of in Chapter IV, provide a moving account of the nature and depth of their disquiet. Rodman comes to the point at once:

At the risk of seeming to deal with Singer's position somewhat as Dr. Johnson dealt with Bishop Berkeley's philosophy, I confess that I need only to stand in the midst of a clear-cut forest, a strip-mined hillside, a defoliated jungle, or a dammed canyon to feel uneasy with assumptions that could yield the conclusion that no human action can make any difference to the welfare of anything but sentient animals. I am agnostic as to whether or not plants, rocks and rivers have subjective experience, and I am not sure that it really matters. I strongly suspect that the same basic principles are manifested in quite diverse forms — e.g. in damming a wild river and repressing an animal instinct (whether human or non-human), in clear-cutting a forest and bombing a city, in Dachau and a university research laboratory, in censoring an idea, liquidating a religious or racial group, and exterminating a species of flora or fauna.[26]

And he continues in this vein:

Singer, like most philosophers and statesmen of the humane movement, represents himself as a stern moralist who disdains the "sentimentality" of little old ladies who fondle pet poodles and write animal shelters into their wills while eating ham sandwiches and wearing cosmetics that were tested on rabbits.[27]

But does the stern moralist disdain sentimentality and eschew speciesism?

In the end, Singer achieves "an expansion of our moral horizons" just far enough to include most animals, with special attention to those categories of animals most appropriate for defining the human condition in the years ahead. The rest of nature is left in a state of thing-hood, having no intrinsic worth, acquiring instrumental value only as resources for the well-being of an elite of sentient beings.[28]

And in a passage that succinctly captures one of my central worries in the present section, Rodman asks:

If it would seem arbitrary to a visitor from Mars to find one species claiming a monopoly of intrinsic value by virtue of its allegedly ex-clusive possession of reason, free will, soul or some other occult qua-lity, would it not seem almost as arbitrary to find that same species claiming a monopoly of intrinsic value for itself and those species most resembling it (e.g. in type of nervous system and behaviour) by virtue of their common and allegedly exclusive possession of sentience? And would not the arbitrariness seem overwhelming if it were then dis-covered that the populations of nonhuman species who were most prominent in this "humane" coalition were what Darwin aptly called "domestic productions", that is, beings produced by the human mani-pulation of nonhuman animal gene pools for human purposes?[29]

I myself am in agreement with this charge of arbitrariness;[30]

---

[26] pp. 89–90.   [27] p. 90.   [28] p. 91.   [29] p. 91.
[30] I must stress that I am not objecting that grounding interests in pain deprives grass and trees of moral rights. If I doubt that human beings and animals have

and I invite the reader to turn back in order to recall how it and the charge of discrimination were earlier prosecuted against those who endow or follow others in endowing pain with moral significance and then use it to define and circum-scribe the class of interest-holders and/or right-holders. What I hope to have conveyed to the reader in the present chapter is that Singer's philosophical case for animal interests collapses, with the result that he has failed to establish his absolutely critical, his absolutely fundamental claim that animals do have interests, upon which his entire case for a moral basis to vegetarianism rests and upon which others, following the Nelsonian argument, have rested their case for animal rights. And with the demise of his case for a *moral* basis to vegetarianism, the use of pain in order to endow animals with moral standing via the notion of interests no longer poses the attraction it at first did. In this way, the very heart and soul of Singer's position is rejected.

Thus, my view remains that the minor premiss of Nelson's argument is false; and this fact bears directly upon those arguments for vegetarianism which essentially involve, if not depend upon, the claim that animals have interests. More-over, the falsity of the minor premiss, together with the dubiousness of the major premiss, ensures that the Nelsonian argument for animal rights fails; and this very failure itself bears upon those arguments for vegetarianism which essen-tially involve, if not depend upon, the claim that animals possess moral rights. In short, though it should be borne in mind that we have not examined all possible analyses of the

---

moral rights, then I am hardly likely to think grass and trees do. My complaint is rather that grounding interests (and/or rights) in pain or other mental states is both discriminatory and arbitrary. It conveniently advantages ourselves and the 'higher' animals and denies moral standing to everything else whatever. My use of the environmentalist (to some, perhaps, a discreditable use) throughout has been to try to bring out this discriminatory and arbitrary character of a mental state view of value and of the position of those, therefore, who use pain to confer interests and/or rights upon animals. The upshot of my arguments in this chapter is that Singer's philosophical case for animal interests can be undermined in such a way as to leave his use of pain as the ground for interests still further exposed. (I am grateful to John Benson for drawing my attention to the need for reiterating this point, to Michael A. Fox for convincing me of its appeal to ecologists, to John Rodman for impressing it upon me so forcefully, and to Singer for dis-cussing the relations of interests and pain with me.)

concept of an interest or all possible arguments for the claim that animals can be the logical subject of rights, nevertheless, in respect of the widely held, centrally important, and significantly influential analysis and argument we have examined, we can conclude that animals have neither interests nor moral rights, with consequent effect upon some alleged moral bases to vegetarianism.

Postscript

I have completed my task: within the confines imposed at the outset of this book, I have argued that animals have neither interests nor moral rights, with consequent effect upon certain alleged moral bases to vegetarianism. Observing these confines, I have rigorously excluded otherwise interesting and important questions about animals — the relative value of animal and human life, the relative value and weight of animal and human suffering, the alleged impossibility of valuing animal suffering without valuing animal life, etc. — which in a more general and less concentrated work would plainly warrant attention. Certainly, a postscript is not the place radically to depart from this rigorous exclusion, nor shall I do so; but there is an implication of something I suggested earlier which the reader may not have drawn and which, even though something of a digression, is perhaps sufficiently important to merit a few, final sentences.

Since Chapter I, I have assumed the truth of the major premiss of Nelson's argument in order to concentrate upon its minor premiss and thereby to meet my opponents on their own ground; but it is my view, as the reader will know from that earlier chapter, that the major premiss of this argument is doubtful, if not false. It implicitly assumes that there are moral rights, and I have tried to show that it is not at all clear that this is so and that we are more than justified in doubting that it is. I shall not reproduce the details of my case here; should it be necessary, the reader can turn back to my arguments to show both that moral rights are superfluous and that we are in no position to affirm that there are any.

The truth is that I am out of sympathy with the present trend of suddenly discovering this or that, which it so happens one has wanted or wanted to be the case all along, to be a moral right, a trend which increasingly knows no bounds, what with the recent formation of pressure groups to lobby and demonstrate on behalf of our moral right to sunshine, a car-free environment, a degree from university (failure produces avoidable mental anguish and often physical distress and so avoidable unhappiness, freedom from which is a right), and a society completely rid of aerosol sprays. So far as I can see, our alleged moral rights proliferate daily; and though some claims to moral rights, such as a moral right to abortion on demand, are obviously much more momentous than others, all such claims, including the momentous ones, presently are foundering in a sea of charges and counter-charges over the existence of moral rights and thereby over the acceptability of the particular normative theses, standards, or principles in which these claims are allegedly grounded and upon which they rely and especially over the adequacy of the normative ethical theories of which these theses etc. form a part.

As I say, I strongly suspect that such claims have become nothing more than means to the end of securing what one or one's group wants; they have become attempts, and not very subtle attempts, to extract by force concessions from those who do not agree with one's view of the rightness or wrongness of this or that. But even where there is agreement in this regard, it by no means follows that there are moral rights lurking somewhere in the shadows: to cite the standard example in this context, I may perfectly well agree and think it right to give part of my salary each month to charities for the poor in London without in the least having to concede that the poor of London have a right to part of my salary.

My conclusion in this book with respect to animal rights, then, may be seen as a part of — certainly, it coheres with — my over-all view about moral rights generally. The implications of this over-all view, however, do not run merely to the denial of moral rights to animals: they extend also, and doubtless more unpalatably, to a denial of moral rights to human beings. And one important thing this means is that we have no moral right to an animal's confinement in zoos, to its ceaseless drudgery and labour on our behalf, to its persistent exploitation in the name of cosmetics, clothing, entertain-

ment, and sport, to its blindness, dismemberment, and ultimate death in the name of science, and, to be sure, to its
appearance on our dining-tables. For anyone with my views,
to pretend otherwise is obviously to be inconsistent, a point
Stephen Clark presses with force and vigour.[1]

On the other hand, it is nonsense to suppose, as many
animal rightists do, that the denial of moral rights to animals
leaves them utterly defenceless; it no more does this than the
denial of a right to abortion on demand leaves a pregnant
woman defenceless. In each case, even on my view, the question of whether our treatment of them is morally right can be
raised and argued; it is not as if, as both Singer and Clark
would agree, the only way we can wrong them is by in-
fringing their putative rights, not as if, for example, Singer's
book or Smart's utilitarianism or Hare's two levels of moral
thinking or my view here must be dismissed out of hand
simply because it does not agree that what makes wrong acts
wrong is that they infringe this or that alleged right. As we
have seen, with no moral rights posited at all, we can still
argue with the feminist about whether it is wrong to deprive
a woman of an abortion when she wants one; even with no
moral rights posited, acts can still be morally wrong, though
we do well to remind ourselves, whatever the pressure from
feminists, animal rightists, and others, that they can also be
morally right. But can animals be wronged, even if they have
no interests? Yes, they can. For I have allowed that the
'higher' animals can suffer unpleasant sensations and so, in
respect of the distinction between harm and hurt, can be
hurt; and wantonly hurting them, just as wantonly hurting
human beings, demands justification, if it is not to be condemned. I do not mean to deny that, even here, fundamental
questions of value will not have to be thrashed out; after all,
one is only going to agree that wantonly hurting animals
amounts to wronging them if one can be brought to agree
that wantonly inflicting unpleasant sensations upon them is
wrong,[2] and, here as elsewhere, simply presenting some un-

---

[1] *The Moral Status of Animals*, pp. 27 ff.

[2] If one does come to agree that wantonly inflicting unpleasant sensations on
animals is wrong, then an opponent may try to circumvent the position on
vegetarianism in this book by seeking to base the moral case for boycotting meat

argued value judgement in this regard is unlikely to bring this about. So, even here, problems may remain; but, importantly, they are not problems about moral rights. The point is that once the question is raised of whether our treatment of animals or our treatment of women is right and/or justified, we begin to set about the task not only of working out acceptable theses of rightness and justification of treatment but also of developing and working out answers to those absolutely critical questions about the adequacy of the normative ethics of which these theses are a part. In a word, we begin to consider the very issues I dubbed in Chapter I the pertinent ones. It is *these* issues which must be argued and established and which appeals to moral rights neither argue nor establish.

On my view, then, questions can still be raised about our treatment of animals; but the answers cannot now consist in appeal to or reliance upon moral rights, claims to which have never really settled questions about our treatment of other creatures anyway.

---

directly upon the pain and suffering animals endure on factory farms, without bringing in any or any explicit concern with interests. I deal with this possibility critically and at length, together with several of the questions referred to above as otherwise important ones excluded here, in a short book entitled 'Modern Moral Vegetarianism: A Critical Assessment', which I am preparing for publication.

Index

Mental States (*cont.*)
as ground for moral rights and
moral standing, 40–52
and utility, 131–2
and value, 46–52
Mill, J. S., 21, 38
Moore, G. E., 14, 38–9, 49
Moral Psychology, 126–7
moral feelings, 127
see also desires, emotions
Moral Rights, 1–2, 4–17, 27, 28–37,
38, 42, 43, 44–7, 50–2, 53,
78–83, 86, 89, 100, 109–10,
139, 158, 159, 163, 164, 166–7,
168–71
and abortion, 10–17, 109–10, 170
animals as logical subject of, 4–8,
18, 27, 28–37, 38–52, 78–83,
88–9, 100, 109–10, 139, 158–
60, 170–1
argument from marginal cases, 22,
28–37, 50, 59, 99–100
argument from potentiality, 22–3,
31
argument from religion, 32
argument from similarity, 31
and choice, 6, 29
and culture, 6, 29, 30
existence of, 6-17, 168–71
and free will, 6, 29, 49
human beings as subject of, 7–17,
28–37, 38–52, 78–83, 109–10,
169–70
and institutional rights, 6n
and lowest common denominator,
51–2
and making claims, 8–17
in law, 8–17
and moral obligations, 6, 29
principles as grounds of, 10–17,
169, 170–1
superfluousness of, 9–12, 17, 169–
71
see also environmental rights/
interests, experiences, interests,
making claims, mental states,
sentiency
Moral Standing, 45–52, 166n
McCloskey, H. J., 5, 6, 18–27, 29
MacKenzie, D. B., 77n

Narveson, J., 28n, 131
Needs, 60–1, 70–7, 81–3, 100, 132n

see also desires, interests, wants
Nelson, L., 5, 6, 53–5, 61, 79, 82, 166,
168
Nelson, W., 9
Nelsonian Argument For Animal
Rights, 5–7, 18, 27, 53, 61, 79,
82, 89, 100, 139, 166–7, 168
Nielsen, K., 131n

Other Minds, Argument From
Analogy, 75n, 84

Pain, *see* Sentiency
Parfit, D., 133n
Passmore, J., 5n, 52n
Pears, D., 62–72, 76, 83
Perception, 118–120
primary perception in plants, 45n
Perlin, S., 146n
Persons, 54, 86, 109–10, 149–51
Plantinga, A., 75n
Pratt, D., 140n
Pratt, V., 124n
Premack, D., 91n, 92n
Prescriptive Meaning, 25–7
and pointlessness, 26–7
Principle of Utility, 131–8
utility, 38–42, 131–2
interpersonal comparisons, 135–6
interspecies comparisons, 136n
Propositions, 87–8, 113–17
see also language, sentences

Quine, W. V. O., 87–8, 114n
see also sentences, propositions
Quinlan, K. A., 146–57, 163
Quinton, A. M., 39

Rashdall, H., 38
Rational Desires, 131–8
see also desires
Rawls, J., 16
Raz, J., 7n
Reasons, 64, 127–30
see also agent-reasons, belief
Regan, T., 5n, 18–27, 28n, 31n, 33n,
35, 38, 55–61, 78, 80n, 109,
159, 160, 161
Rembrandt, 72, 79–80
Rights, *see* Moral Rights
Robinson, H. M., 89n
Rodman, J., 9n, 28n, 42n, 43, 44, 46,
51–2, 164–5, 166n